Contents

Focus on Vocab

Being Young: Life at Home and Abroad 6
Ready, Steady, Go? – The Experience of Work 18
Courting the Consumer: Between Sales and Services 28
Making Yourself Understood – The English Language in Use 39
Do We Get What We Deserve? – Personal Identities and Social Relationships 45
Learning for Life? Lifelong Learning? – Teaching, Learning and Education 57
A World on the Move: Global Migration and Mobility 69
Technology and Society: Steam, Steel and Science 81
Technological Progress and Responsibility – (Green) Technology to Save the World? 93
The Global Challenge – Economy Worldwide 106
All the World's a Stage: Art and Literature 118
The Culture Industry: Perception, Persuasion & Promises in the Media 125

Specialist Vocab

Advertising Terms 133
Business, Administration & Finance 139
Science & Technology 143
Information Technology 147
Education & Social Affairs 150
Art & Design 154

Focus on Facts

The Function of Marketing and Marketing Instruments 156
Factors of the Market Economy 158
Consumer Protection and Protection Authorities 160
Trade Unions 162
The Challenge of Demographic Change 164
Human Needs 166
Immigration and Minorities in the United States 168
Great Britain – A Multicultural Society 170
The Industrial Revolution 174
Genetic Engineering 176
The European Union 178
Global Economy 180
Globalisation 182
World Trade 184
Drama and Theatre 186
The Media 188
The Press 190

Focus on Skills

Analysis of a Fictional Text 192
Analysis of a Non-Fictional Text 194
Analysis of Poetry and Lyrics/Songs 196
Analysis of a Political Speech 198
Basic Types of Fictional Texts 200
Basic Types of Non-Fictional Texts 202
Characterization of a Figure in Literature 204
Commercial Correspondence – Business Letter 206
Commercial Correspondence – Enquiry 208
Commercial Correspondence – Offer 210

Commercial Correspondence – Order 212
Commercial Correspondence – Complaint (The Seller) 214
Commercial Correspondence – Complaint (The Buyer) 216
Giving a Speech 218
Job Interview 220
Telephoning: Making/Taking a Telephone Call 226
Writing a CV and a Letter of Application 234
Writing a Letter to the Editor 236
Writing a Management Summary and an Abstract 238
Writing a Comment and a Review 240
Writing – Summary/Essay/Creative Writing 242

Focus on Language

Vocabulary and Phrases for Text Analysis 244

Thematic and Vocab Index 248

Note: This * sign indicates that the word/term can be found in the *Glossary of Literary Terms* in your Students' Book

Being Young: Life at Home and Abroad

English word/phrase	Explanation in English	German equivalent and/or synonym(s)
	youth culture	
adolescence [ˌædəˈlesns]	the period during which a young person develops into an adult	*Jugend*
adolescent	a young person between the age of 12 and 18	*Jugendliche(r)*
youth	the time of life when sb. is young, esp. the time before a child becomes an adult; a teenage boy (*plural* **youths**)	*Jugend(zeit)*
to criticize sb./sth.	to express your disapproval of sb./sth.	*jdn. kritisieren*
(non)conformity	behaviour that (doesn't obey) obeys the accepted rules of society	*(Un-)Angepasstheit (an gesellschaftliche Normen und Regeln)*
deviant (behaviour) [ˈdiːviənt]	differing, often in a bad way, from what is considered normal behaviour	*von der Norm abweichendes Verhalten*
difference of opinion	a slight disagreement	*Meinungsverschiedenheit, Streit*
grown-up *(adj.)*	fully developed; behaving in a responsible way	*reif/erwachsen;* mature
grown-up *(n.)*	an adult	*Erwachsene(r)*
to hang out *(infml.)*	to spend a lot of time in a particular place with particular people	*abhängen, rumhängen mit jdm.*

identity [aɪˈdentəti]	the qualities and attitudes a person or group has/have that make them different from other people	*Identität*
to lose one's temper	to suddenly become very angry	*die Geduld/Nerven verlieren*
mature	fully grown and developed; behaving in a sensible and reasonable way	*reif/erwachsen;* grown-up
puberty	the period of a person's life in which their sexual organs develop and they become capable of having children	*Pubertät*
to pursue an interest	to willingly devote time and attention to sth.	*ein Anliegen (zielstrebig) verfolgen*
to question sb./sth.	to have doubts about whether sth./sb. is good	*etwas/jdn. infrage stellen*
to rebel (against sb./sth.) [rɪˈbel]	to oppose or to fight against sb. in authority/an idea/a situation which you do not agree with	*rebellieren (gegen)*
role model	sb. people admire and whose behaviour they try to copy	*Idol*
to surf the Internet	to look quickly through information on the Internet for anything that interests you	*im Internet surfen/nach Informationen suchen*
teenage(d)	aged between 13 and 18	*jugendlich*

teenager	a person between 13 and 18	*Jugendliche(r)*
youthful	typical of young people	*jugendlich*
youth (sub-)culture	the interests and activities of young people	*Jugendkultur*

English word/phrase	Explanation in English	German equivalent and/or synonym(s)
	teenage pregnancy	
(to have an) abortion	(to have) a medical operation to end a pregnancy	*eine Abtreibung (vornehmen lassen)*
to be in love	to develop a strong (sexual) feeling for sb.	*sich verlieben*
to be heartbroken	to be extremely sad because of sth. that has happened	*todunglücklich, untröstlich sein; unglücklich verliebt sein*
to be jealous of sb./ sth.	feeling angry and unhappy because sb. you like is showing interest in another person or sb. has sth. you want to have	*eifersüchtig/neidisch auf jdn./etwas sein*
to be on the pill	taking a hormone pill regularly in order not to get pregnant	*die (Anti-Baby-) Pille nehmen*
birth control	the practice of controlling the number of children a person has, using various methods of contraception	*Geburtenkontrolle, -regelung*

(the use of) contraception	the practice/methods of preventing a woman from getting pregnant	*Schwangerschaftsverhütung (anwenden)*
contraceptive	a drug, object or method used to prevent a woman from becoming pregnant	*Verhütungsmittel*
counselling (on pregnancy options)	advice and support given by a counsellor to sb. with problems, e.g. an unwanted pregnancy etc.	*Schwangerschaftskonfliktberatung*
to date sb.	to go out with sb.	*sich mit jdm. verabreden, mit jdm. ausgehen*
to enjoy sb.'s company	to love to see/meet/be with sb.	*jmds. Gesellschaft genießen*
to have sex with sb.	to have sexual intercourse with sb.	*Sex/Geschlechtsverkehr mit jdm. haben*
helpline	a telephone number that you can ring if you need advice	*Sorgentelefon*
to make love to sb.	to have sex with sb.	*Sex/Geschlechtsverkehr mit jdm. haben*
mutual	mutual feelings are feelings that two or more people have for each other	*gegenseitig*
pregnancy test	a medical test that shows if a woman is pregnant or not	*Schwangerschaftstest*
premarital (sex)	(having sex) before marriage	*vorehelicher (Geschlechtsverkehr)*

promiscuity	the situation of having many sexual partners	*häufiger (Geschlechts-) Partnerwechsel*
promiscuous [prəˈmɪskjuəs]	having many sexual partners	*häufig den (Geschlechts-) Partner wechselnd*
to quit a relationship	to end a relationship	*eine Beziehung beenden*
relationship	an emotional and/or sexual liaison/affair	*Beziehung*
(to practise) safe sex	sexual activity in which people try to protect themselves from AIDS and other sexual diseases, for example by using a condom	*Safer Sex praktizieren (indem man Kondome benutzt, um sich vor Geschlechtskrankeiten oder Aids zu schützen)*
(to have) sexual intercourse	the physical activity of two people having sex with each other	*Geschlechtsverkehr (haben)*
(sexual) maturity	the age when a person is able to reproduce; puberty	*(sexuelle) Reife*
STD (sexually transmitted disease)	a disease or infection that is transmitted by having sex with sb.	*Geschlechtskrankheit*

English word/phrase	Explanation in English	German equivalent and/or synonym(s)
initiation • partnership • peer group		
to achieve sth.	to successfully complete sth.	*etwas erreichen*
achievement	sth. important that you succeed in doing	*Errungenschaft/Ziel, das man erreicht hat*
age of majority	the age when sb. legally becomes an adult	*Volljährigkeit*

to aim to do sth.	to try or intend to achieve sth.	*etwas beabsichtigen zu tun*
to enter a new phase	to start sth. new in one's life	*einen neuen Lebens-abschnitt beginnen*
eligibility [ˌelɪdʒəˈbɪlati]	the state of being able or allowed to do sth. because you are at the right age	*Berechtigung*
to vote/to be eligible to vote	being legally allowed to vote	*berechtigt sein, zu wählen*
to experiment with sth.	to try using various ideas, methods to find out how good they are	*mit etwas experimen-tieren/etwas auspro-bieren*
femininity [ˌfeməˈnɪnəti]	qualities that are considered to be typical of women, esp. gentleness, delicate-ness and prettiness	*Weiblichkeit, Femininität*
to gain experience	to gradually get more and more knowledge and skills	*Erfahrung(en) sammeln*
gang/a gang of youths	a group of young people who spend time together and who are often involved in crime or drugs and fight against other groups	*Jugendbande*
to get through sth.	to come successfully to the end of a difficult time	*etwas hinter sich bringen*
initiation [ɪˌnɪʃiˈeʃn]	introducing a young person to adult life, often with a ceremony	*Initiation, Eintritt in das Erwachsensein*

legal emancipation	having the legal rights and responsibilities of an adult person	*rechtliche Gleichberechtigung*
masculinity [ˌmæskju'lɪnəti]	qualities that are considered to be typical of men, esp. strength, muscularity, etc.	*Maskulinität, Männlichkeit*
peer group/peer(s)	people who are the same age as you	*altersgleiche Jugendliche*
peer pressure	a strong feeling that you must do the same things as other people of your age	*Gruppenzwang, Gruppendruck*
puberty	the period of a person's life in which their sexual organs develop and they become capable of having children	*Pubertät*
pubescent [pjuː'besnt]	being in the state of going through puberty	*pubertierend*
to search for one's own identity	the act of trying to find out who you are/what your abilities/qualities are	*seine Identität suchen; herausfinden, wer man ist*
socialization	the process by which sb., esp. a child, learns to behave in a socially acceptable way	*Sozialisation, Vergesellschaftung*
to team up with sb.	to join with sb. in order to work on sth.	*mit jdm. zusammenarbeiten*
transition	when sth. changes from one form to another	*Übergang, Wechsel*

English word/phrase	Explanation in English	German equivalent and/or synonym(s)
	violence • drugs	
addiction	the condition of being unable to stop taking drugs, alcohol, etc. or doing sth. as a habit	*Abhängigkeit*
to be addicted (to sth./sb.)	being unable to stop doing sth.	*abhängig sein*
aggression	angry or threatening behaviour or feelings that often result in fighting	*Aggression, Gewalttätigkeit*
alcoholic *(n.)*	a person who regularly drinks too much alcohol and cannot easily stop drinking	*Alkoholiker(in)*
alcoholism	the medical condition of being an alcoholic	*Alkoholismus, Alkoholabhängigkeit*
anger	a strong feeling of wanting to hurt or criticize sb. because they have done sth. unkind to you	*Wut*
to be in a bad temper	to be in a bad mood	*schlechte Laune haben*
binge drinking	the act of drinking a large amount of alcohol in a short time in order to get drunk	*Saufgelage*
to bully sb.	to threaten to hurt sb. who is smaller or weaker	*jdn. tyrannisieren, schikanieren*
bullying *(n.)*	the act of threatening or hurting a weaker person	*tyrannisieren, schikanieren (von einem Schwächeren)*

drug abuse	the practice of drinking too much or taking illegal drugs	*Drogenmissbrauch*
to do sth. to excess	to do sth. too much so that it may harm you more than is reasonable	*etwas im Übermaß tun*
frightening	making you feel afraid	*angst-/furchteinflößend*
habit	sth. that you do regularly, often without thinking about it	*Gewohnheit*
habit-forming	causing you to want to keep doing or taking sth., e.g. a drug	*gewohnheitsprägend*
miserable	extremely unhappy	*elend*
out of/under control	(not) having the power to make sth./sb. do what you want	*außer/unter Kontrolle*
physical violence	hitting or beating sb.	*körperliche Gewalt*
to take drugs	to consume drugs	*Drogen nehmen*
to tempt sb. to do sth.	to make sb. want to have or do sth. even though they know they really should not	*jdn. zu etwas verführen*
to threaten sb.	to say that you will harm sb. if they do not do what you want	*jdn. bedrohen*
the thrill (of a lifetime)	the excitement of doing sth.	*der besondere Reiz von etwas*
to throw up/to vomit	to eject the contents of your stomach out through your mouth because you feel ill	*sich übergeben*

victim	sb. who has been attacked, robbed or murdered	*Opfer*
violation (of rules)	an action that breaks a law	*Gesetzesbruch/-verstoß*

English word/phrase	Explanation in English	German equivalent and/or synonym(s)
anorexia • obesity		
anorexia	mental illness that makes sb. avoid eating	*Magersucht*
anorexic	suffering from anorexia	*magersüchtig*
appearance	the way sb. looks to other people	*(äußere) Erscheinung*
(physical) attractive-ness	the quality of being good looking	*Attraktivität, gutes Aussehen*
to be a particular weight	how heavy and fat sb. is	*ein bestimmtes Gewicht haben*
big	when sb. has a large body	*dick*
to binge on sth.	to eat or drink too much, esp. without being able to control yourself	*übermäßig essen oder trinken*
BMI (body mass index)	the relationship between your height and your weight	*das Verhältnis zwischen Körpergröße und Gewicht*
body weight	how heavy your body is	*Körpergewicht*
bulimia	an illness in which a person cannot stop eating too much, and then vomits in order to control their weight	*Ess-Brechsucht, Bulimie*

chubby	slightly fat in a nice-looking way (babies)	*pummelig*
eating disorder	mental condition in which you do not eat a normal amount of food	*Essstörung*
eating habit(s)	the practice of what or how sb. eats	*Essgewohnheiten*
fat	weighing too much	*übergewichtig*
fat intake	the amount of fat you eat	*Fettaufnahme, -zufuhr*
to gain/lose weight	to increase/decrease how heavy you are	*zunehmen/abnehmen*
to get/keep your weight down	to lose weight	*sein Gewicht reduzieren*
good-looking	attractive	*gutaussehend, attraktiv*
handsome	good-looking (man)	*gutaussehend, attraktiv*
sb.'s ideal weight	the weight that is healthy and best for sb.	*Idealgewicht*
image (of sb.)	a picture that you have in your mind, esp. about what sb./sth. is like or the way they look	*(geistige) Vorstellung von jdm./etwas haben*
obese [əʊˈbiːs]	extremely fat in a way that is dangerous to your health	*fettleibig*
obesity	when sb. is very fat in a way that is unhealthy	*Fettleibigkeit, extremes Übergewicht*
plus-size	euphemistic for fat or obese	*Übergröße*

role model	sb. whose behaviour, attitudes, etc. people try to copy because they admire them	*Idol*
skinny	very thin	*mager*
slim	attractively thin	*schlank;* slender
to starve oneself	to eat very little food in order to become thinner	*(sich schlank) hungern*
tall	of more than average height	*groß, lang*
underweight	weighing less than is expected or usual	*untergewichtig*
to watch your weight	to be careful (e.g. by eating not too much) in order not to gain any weight	*auf sein Gewicht achten*
well-being	feeling of being happy and healthy	*Wohlgefühl*
well-built	sb. who is well-built has a big, strong body	*gut gebaut*

Ready, Steady, Go? – The Experience of Work

English word/phrase	Explanation in English	German equivalent and/or synonym(s)
	work	
to apply for (a job)	to make a formal request for sth.	*sich (für eine Stelle) bewerben*
applicant	sb. who applies for a job	*Bewerber(in)*
application	a formal (written) request for a job	*Bewerbung*
apprenticeship	the period of time in which a (young) person works for an employer in order to learn the particular skills needed for the job	*Ausbildung; Lehre*
basic requirement	a fundamental quality that sb./sth. has to have to meet a certain standard/sb.'s expectations	*Grundvoraussetzung*
blind (unsolicited) application	enquiry about the possibility of a job even though one hasn't been advertised	*Blindbewerbung (auf eine nicht ausgeschriebene Stelle)*
CEO [ˌsiː iː ˈəʊ] (chief executive officer)	the person with the highest rank in the company	*Geschäftsführer(in)*
commercial correspondence	the act of writing and receiving letters/emails, etc. in connection with business	*Geschäftskorrespondenz*

competitive	trying hard to be better than others	*ehrgeizig;* ambitious
(to make a) complaint	a formal statement in which sb. complains about sth.	*Beschwerde; Reklamation*
computer literacy	ability to use a computer	*mit einem Computer umgehen können*
corporate image	the image of a company that all its members should display to the public	*Unternehmensphilosophie, das Ansehen eines Unternehmens*
craftsmanship	very detailed work that has been done using a lot of skill, to make sth. beautiful with one's hands	*Handwerk; handwerkliches Können*
CV (Curriculum Vitae) *(BE)*	a short written document that outlines sb's education and previous jobs	*Lebenslauf;* résumé *(US)*
to employ sb.	to give sb. a job	*jdn. anstellen/ beschäftigen*
employee	a person who is paid to work for sb.	*Angestellte(r)*
employer	a person, company or organization that employs people	*Arbeitgeber*
employment legislation	the laws connected with work, workers, etc.	*Arbeitsrecht*
enquiry [ɪnˈkwaɪəri]	the act or process of asking questions in order to get information	*Anfrage; Erhebung*

expert knowledge	a special skill or knowledge of a subject	*Fachwissen; Expertenwissen*
to freelance	to earn money by selling your work to many different companies/organizations	*selbstständig/ freiberuflich tätig sein*
to gain work experience	to get experience in a particular job	*Arbeitserfahrung machen*
home working	work done at home; often jobs that are not well-paid, such as making clothes for shops, etc.	*Heimarbeit*
ICT (Information and Communications Technology)	term that stresses the unified communications and telecommunications that enable users to access, store, transmit and manipulate information	*Informations- und Kommunikationstechnik*
job advert/offer	an advertisement published by a company to find new employees	*Stellenanzeige*
job interview	interview held by a company to find out about a potential new employee's qualifications and motivation	*Vorstellungsgespräch*
job market	the people looking for work and the number of jobs that are available	*Arbeitsmarkt*

key qualifications	the relevant skills sb. is expected to have for a specific job, e.g. professional experience, foreign languages, academic degrees, etc.	*Schlüssel-qualifikationen*
letter of application	letter that sb. writes to a company to apply for a job	*Bewerbungsschreiben*
manufacturing	the business or industry of producing goods in large quantities in factories, etc.	*Fabrikation; Produktion; Fertigung*
office work	work done in an office, e.g. as a secretary, etc.	*Büroarbeit*
open-plan office	a building or area that does not have walls dividing it up into rooms	*Großraumbüro*
professional skills	specific skills that are required for any person who is working; you gain these skills through job experience or taking courses, etc.	*berufliche Kompetenzen*
qualification(s)	a skill or type of experience that you need for a particular job	*Qualifikation, Fähigkeit(en)*
to recruit sb./ recruitment	to find new people to join a company	*Jdn. anwerben/ einstellen; Anwerbung/ Einstellung*
to renew a contract	to extend a contract	*einen (Arbeits-)Vertrag erneuern/verlängern*

requirement	a quality or ability you must have in order to do sth. else	*Voraussetzung; Anforderung*
résumé *(US)* [rɪ'zjuːm]	a short written document that outlines your education and previous jobs	*Lebenslauf*
retiree [rɪˌtaɪə'ri]	sb. who has stopped working, usually because of age	*Pensionär, Rentner*
retirement	the period after you have stopped work	*Ruhestand; Pensionierung*
to retrain	to learn a new type of work/a new skill	*umschulen*
(un)skilled	(not) having special training/qualifications	*(un-)gelernt, (un-) ausgebildet*
semi-skilled	having some special training/qualifications but less than skilled people	*angelernt (d. h. mit Berufskenntnissen, aber ohne Abschluss)*
skill	an ability to do sth. well, esp. because you have learned and practised it	*Fähigkeit; Fertigkeit*
social skills	any skill encouraging and supporting interaction and communication with others	*soziale Kompetenz*
soft skills	social skills such as interaction and communication with others	*soziale Kompetenz*

(to work as a) substitute	a person that works instead of the person who normally does the job	*Ersatz; Aushilfe*
placement	a job, usually as part of a course or study, which gives you experience of a particular type of work	*Praktikantenstelle*
teleworking	a job in which sb. works from home, and communicates with their employer, customers, etc. using a computer, telephone, etc.	*Telearbeit; Heimarbeitsplatz*
temporary work	work continuing only for a limited period of time	*Zeitarbeit; vorübergehende Beschäftigung; Leiharbeit*
unfair dismissal	the act of removing sb. from his/her job without justified reasons	*ungerechtfertigte Entlassung*
vocational training	training connected with a job	*Berufsschulsausbildung*
wide-span factory shed	a big building which is not divided by walls in which goods are produced	*Großraumfabrikationshalle*
working environment	the people and things that are around you at work	*Arbeitsumgebung*
work experience	the time that you have worked in a particular job and gained skills	*Berufserfahrung*
to work part-time	to work for part of the day or week	*halbtags/in Teilzeit arbeiten*

English word/phrase	Explanation in English	German equivalent and/or synonym(s)
	volunteerism	
after-school tutoring	getting private lessons from a teacher after school	*Hausaufgabenbetreuung, Privatunterricht, Nachhilfe*
allegiance [a'liːdʒans]	a person's continued support for sth./sb.	*Treue, Zustimmung, Unterstützung*
call to service	a strong feeling that you want to work for your community, etc.	*den Drang/Wunsch haben, sich sozial zu engagieren*
civil service	the non-military government service departments in a country, e.g. social workers	*Staatsdienst*
community service	work helping people in the local community that sb. does without being paid	*Freiwilligendienst*
Foreign Service	Diplomatic Service	*Diplomatischer Dienst*
gap year	a year that a young person spends working or travelling, usually between leaving school and starting university	*freiwilliges (soziales) Jahr*
to meet common challenges	to have the qualities that are commonly required/expected	*den allgemeinen Bedürfnissen/ Anforderungen entsprechen*
to mentor sb.	to help and advise a person with less experience	*jdn. betreuen/beraten*
to take/to seize an/ the opportunity	to do sth. you have a chance to do	*die Gelegenheit ergreifen*

to participate in sth.	to take part in sth.	*an etwas teilnehmen*
public service	a service, such as transport or health, that a government provides for people	*öffentlicher Dienst*
to serve a common purpose	to do sth. in order to help and support others	*dem Gemeinwohl dienen*
social commitment	the willingness to work hard and give your energy and time for social purposes	*soziales Engagement*
voluntary	done willingly, not because you are forced or paid to do it	*freiwillig*
volunteer	a person who does a job without being paid for it	*sich freiwillig melden*

English word/phrase	Explanation in English	German equivalent and/or synonym(s)
	going abroad	
to apply for a visa	to make a formal request for permis-sion to enter a foreign country	*ein Visum beantragen*
certificate of vaccination	an official document that shows a person's vaccinations/immun-izations against certain diseases	*Impfpass*
cross-cultural communication	communication involving ideas from different countries/cultures	*interkulturelle Verständigung*
cultural immersion	the state of being completely involved in a new culture	*kulturelle Verschmel-zung*

exchange student	a student who visits another school or university to work or study while a student from that school/university attends his/her school/university	*Austauschschüler(in)*
foreign currency	a different system of money than the one that is used in one's own country	*ausländische (Geld-) Währung*
to get a briefing	to be in a short meeting in which people are given instructions or information	*Instruktionen/ Anweisungen bekommen*
international volunteering	going abroad for voluntary work	*internationaler Freiwilligendienst*
outreach programme	the activity of an organization that provides a service or advice for people in the community who would be unlikely to come to an official office	*Vor-Ort-Einsatz/ -Programm*
reverse culture shock	shock/difficulty that people have in adapting when they come home from a stay abroad	*Anpassungsprobleme/ Wiedereingliederungsprobleme nach einem Auslandsaufenthalt*
safety precautions	measures that sb. takes to ensure a safe environment/ situation	*Sicherheitsvorkehrungen*
to settle back in	to get used to your home again	*sich wieder heimisch fühlen*
stay abroad	stay in a foreign country	*Auslandsaufenthalt*

to study abroad	to go to a school or university in a foreign country	*Auslandsstudium*
to travel overseas	to travel to a foreign country	*eine Auslandsreise machen*

English word/phrase	Explanation in English	German equivalent and/or synonym(s)
	charity	
charity organization	an organization that gives money, goods or help to people who are poor, sick, etc.	*Wohlfahrtsorganisation*
charitable	helping people who are poor or in need	*menschenfreundlich, gütig*
to donate/give sth. to charity	to give money, food, clothes, etc. to charity	*etwas für gemeinnützige Zwecke spenden*
to be engaged in sth.	to be busy doing sth.	*mit etwas beschäftigt sein*
to finance a project	to give money to enable a project to operate	*ein Projekt finanzieren/ unterstützen*
living conditions	the external aspects of the situation that people live in	*Lebensbedingungen*
to meet sb.'s basic needs	to make sure that sb.'s basic needs (= food, water, shelter, etc.) are satisfied and taken care of	*jdns. Grundbedürfnissen gerecht werden*
NGO (non-governmental organization)	a charity organization that is inde-pendent of government and business	*Hilfsorganisation*
to take advantage of sth.	to use the opportunities that you have	*Gelegenheiten wahrnehmen/nutzen*

Courting the Consumer: Between Sales and Services

English word/phrase	Explanation in English	German equivalent and/or synonym(s)
	marketing • advertising	
to address sb.	to say sth. directly to sb.	*jdn. dirket ansprechen; addressieren*
advertisement/ad	a public notice, designed to present goods, in which the sponsor is identified	*Werbung/ Werbeanzeige*
A I D A (abbr./ acronym)	(gain) **A**ttention (hold) **I**nterest (arouse) **D**esire (encourage to take) **A**ction	*Werbeformel: Aufmerksamkeit, Interesse, Begierde, (Kauf-) Handlung*
to appeal to sb./ appealing	to make a product attractive, interesting	*jdn. Ansprechen, jds. Interesse wecken*
to attract sb.'s attention	to make sb. interested in sth.	*jds. Aufmerksamkeit erwecken*
audiovisual presen-tation	a presentation involving both pictures and spoken words	*audio-visuelle Darstellung*
B & W	black and white ad	*Schwarz-Weiß-Werbe-anzeige*
bold; heavy-faced type	in a thick, dark type	*Fettdruck*
billboard/billboard advertising	advertising on a large board on the outside of a building or at the side of the road	*große Reklamefläche*
body copy	the main part of the reading matter	*(Haupt-) Werbetext*
brand	the label by which a product is identified	*Marke; Markenname*

brand image/ personality	the pattern of feelings, ideas and images held by the public with regard to a specific brand	*Markenansehen; Markenprofil*
brand loyalty	the tendency of customers to continue buying the same product	*Produkttreue*
caption	text written underneath a picture to explain it	*Bildlegende*
client ['klaɪənt]	customer	*Kunde*
column	one of the vertical sections in which the printed page of a book, newspaper, etc. is divided	*Textspalte*
competition/ competitor	a situation in which people or organizations compete with each other	*Wettbewerb(er)*
consumer advertising	advertising of products sold to the general public	*Konsumentenwerbung*
to convince sb.	to make sb. believe that sth. is true	*jdn. überzeugen*
copy	any word or text material for publication, broadcast or production	*Abbildung; Kopie; Abzug*
copywriter	a person who writes advertisements	*Werbetexter*
editor	a person who is in charge of a newspaper, etc.	*Herausgeber*

to evoke interest in sth.	to cause interest in sth.	*Interesse erwecken*
eye-catcher	sth. that is immediately noticeable because it is particularly interesting	*Blickfang*
eye appeal	sth. that attracts people's attention	*Werbewirksamkeit*
front page	first page of a newspaper/magazine	*Titelseite; Aufmacher*
four colour	artwork reproduced in full colour	*vierfarbig; Farbdruck*
label	a piece of paper, etc. that is attached to sth. and that gives information about it; tag	*Etikett; Beschriftung*
merchandising	activities designed to promote retail sales	*Merchandising; Absatzförderung*
to persuade sb.	to make sb. agree to do/believe sth. by giving them good reasons	*jdn. überreden/ überzeugen*
persuasive [pə'sweɪsɪv]	being able to make sb. do/believe sth.	*überzeugend*
prime time	peak viewing time; time when the greatest number of people are watching TV/listening to the radio, etc.	*Haupteinschaltzeit; Hauptsendezeit*
press release/ news release	written news information mailed to the media	*Pressemitteilung*
promotion	activities used to encourage the purchase of a product	*Werbung; Verkaufsförderung*

psychographics	statistics relating to the personalities, attitudes and life-styles of people and used as a tool in marketing	*Verbraucherforschung*
public relations (PR)	practice of influencing the press so that they print stories that promote a company/ product	*Öffentlichkeitsarbeit*
research	careful study of a subject in order to discover new facts/ information	*Recherche; Nach-forschung*
to seduce sb. [sɪ'djuːs]	to persuade sb. to do sth. that they would not usually agree to do by making it seem very attractive; to entice	*jdn. verführen*
seduction [sɪ'dʌkʃn]	the act of enducing enticement	*Verführung;* enticement
slogan	a word or phrase that is easy to remember esp. in advertising	*Slogan; Werbespruch*
subconscious(ly) [ˌsʌb'kɑnʃəsli]	connected with feelings that influence your behaviour even though you are not aware of them	*unterbewusst*
subheadline/-heading	title given to a part of an article	*Unterzeile*
supplement	an extra separate section that is sold with the newspaper/ magazine	*Beiheft; Beilage*

sweepstakes	a sales promotion in which prizes are awarded to the customer	*Wettspiel*
target group	a particular group of people the advertisement is aimed at	*Zielgruppe*
trade advertising	advertising aimed at wholesalers, distributors and retailers rather than customers	*Branchenwerbung; Händlerwerbung*
trademark (TM)	name, symbol or design a company uses for its products and that cannot be used by anyone else	*Handelsmarke; Warenzeichen*
two colour	ad printed in two colours, usually black and a second colour for effect	*zweifarbig; Zweifarbigkeit*
unconscious(ly)	without being aware	*unbewusst*

English word/phrase	Explanation in English	German equivalent and/or synonym(s)
consumer protection		
advertising standards authority	a self-regulatory organisation of the advertising industry in the UK	*Organisation der Werbewirtschaft zur Festlegung von Werbestandards*
civil law	law that deals with the rights of private citizens rather than with crime	*Bürgerliches Gesetzbuch*
commercial code	laws and acts relating to trade and sales	*Handelsgesetzbuch*

competition regulation	law that promotes or maintains market competition	*Wettbewerbsregelung*
(to deal with a) complaint	statement sb. (e.g. a customer) makes saying that they are not satisfied	*sich mit einer Beschwerde beschäftigen; sich darum kümmern*
consumer advice institution	organization that informs consumers and gives practical advice	*Verbraucherratgeber-institution*
consumer protection	laws and organizations to ensure the rights of consumers	*Verbraucherschutz*
consumer rights	rights of consumers to be protected against fraud and unfair business practices	*Verbraucherrechte*
credit repair/debit repair	authority that helps people to manage their debts	*Kredit-/Schuldnerberatung*
food safety	scientific discipline describing handling, preparation, and storage of food in ways that prevent foodborne illness	*Lebensmittelsicherheit*
fraud [frɔːd]	the crime of cheating sb.	*Betrug*
marketplace	the activity of competing with other companies to buy and sell goods, services, etc.	*Marktplatz; Markt*

privacy ['prɪvəsi] *(BE)* ['praɪvəsi] *(US)* **rights**	the right of being free from the attention of the public	*Rechte zum Schutz der Privatsphäre*
product liability	the state of being legally responsible for a product	*Produkthaftung*
to protect sb. from sth.	to make sure that sb. is not harmed, injured, damaged, etc.	*jdn. vor etw. schützen*
service and sales contracts	legal contracts on the exchange of goods, properties and services between seller and buyer	*Dienstleistungs- und Verkaufsverträge*
trustworthy	worthy of being depended on; reliable	*vertrauenswürdig*
unfair business practices	acts connected with fraud, misrepresentation of consumers	*unfaire/unlautere Geschäftspraktiken*
watchdog	a person or group of people whose job is to check that companies are not doing anything illegal or violating people's rights	*Regulierungsbehörde*

English word/phrase	Explanation in English	German equivalent and/or synonym(s)
consumerism • consumption		
acquisition of sth.	the act of buying sth.	*Anschaffung, Erwerb*
availability	the fact that someone is free to work, be contacted, etc, or whether or how much they can	*Verfügbarkeit*

(to be) available (to sb.)	able to be reached by sb.	*erhältlich, verfügbar*
to cash a paycheck	to exchange a cheque for the amount of money it is worth	*einen Gehaltsscheck einlösen*
consumer	someone who buys and uses products and services	*Konsument*
customer	someone who buys goods or services from a shop, company etc	*Kunde*
discount shopping	to go shopping at a store that sells goods cheaply	*im Discount einkaufen*
to display sth.	to present sth.	*etw. zeigen*
distribution of sth.	the act of sharing things among a large group of people	*Verteilung*
efficiency	the quality of doing sth. well without wasting money or time	*Effizienz, Leistungs-fähigkeit*
industrialized mass production	when products are made in large numbers by industrial machines so they can be sold cheaply	*industrialisierte Massenproduktion*
to instil a desire	to put the idea in sb.'s mind, that they desire sth.	*jdm. eine Begierde einflößen*
Internet retailer	Internet shop	*Internethändler*
to line the shelves	to offer sth. for sale in large amounts	*den Absatz steigern*
mounting consumer debt	strongly rising consumer debt	*steigende Konsum-verschuldung*

online shopping portal	a website where you can buy things online	*online Einkaufsportal*
price spiral [spaɪrəl]	a rise in prices	*Preisspirale*
purchasing power	the amount of money a person or group has available to spend	*Kaufkraft*
shipping	the delivery of goods esp. by ship	*Lieferung, Verschiffung*
status symbol	sth. that you have or own that shows high social rank or position	*Statussymbol*
range of products	selection of products	*Produktumfang*
retailer/retail store	a person or store that sells goods	*Händler, Einzelhändler*

English word/phrase	Explanation in English	German equivalent and/or synonym(s)
trade unions • labour policy		
annual holidays	the holidays an employee can take per year	*Jahresurlaub*
benefit	extra money or other advantages that you get as a part of your job	*freiwillige/zusätzliche Leistung*
company board	board of directors and leading managers of a company	*Aufsichtsrat*
company pension plan	a system in which the employer and the employee pay regularly into a retirement fund during employment	*betriebliche Altersvor-sorge*
to dismiss	to officially remove sb. from their job	*entlasssen*

employment legislation	laws that govern the employer/employee relations and right of employees	*Arbeitsgesetzgebung; -gesetze*
(to go) freelance	earning money by selling your work to several different organizations rather than being employed by one employer	*freiberuflich arbeiten*
(to work) flexitime	system in which employees work a particular number of hours each week/month but can choose when they start and finish work	*gleitende Arbeitszeit; Gleitzeit*
(to work) full-time	all the hours of a week/month during which people normally work	*Vollzeit-; in Vollzeit*
labour contract	contract between employee and employer	*Arbeitsvertrag*
labour market	the number of people who are available for work in relation to the number of jobs available	*Arbeitsmarkt*
to lay off (laid off, laid off)	to make people unemployed because there is no more work	*entlassen*
(to work) overtime	to work extra hours	*Überstunden; Mehrarbeit*
(to work) part-time	a part of the day/week in which people work	*Teilzeit-; in Teilzeit*

paternity/maternity leave	paid time that the parents of a new baby are allowed to have away from work	*Erziehungsurlaub*
personnel	the people who work for an organisation	*Personal*
salary	money employees get for their work	*(Jahres-/Monats-) Gehalt*
to (go on) strike	to refuse to work in order to protest against sth.	*streiken*
unemployment benefit	money paid by the government to sb. who is unemployed	*Arbeitslosenunterstützung*
(trade) union	organization of workers to protect their interests	*Gewerkschaft*
wages *(pl.)*	money people earn for work/service	*Lohn; Löhne*
works council	group of employees who represent all the employees of a company	*Betriebsrat*
workforce	all the people working for a company	*Arbeiterschaft*

Making Yourself Understood – The English Language in Use

English word/phrase	Explanation in English	German equivalent and/or synonym(s)
language • communication		
acronym	a word formed from the first letters of the words that make up the name of sth., e.g. UN (United Nations)	*Akronym, Kurzwort*
bilingual [ˌbaiˈlɪŋgwəl]	with a command of two languages	*zweisprachig*
colloquial	used in conversation but not in formal speech or writing	*umgangssprachlich*
colloquialism	an expression or word used in informal conversation	*umgangssprachlicher Ausdruck*
communication model(s)	conceptual model(s) used to explain the human communication process	*Kommunikationsmodell*
communicative competence	a person's awareness of the rules governing the appropriate use of language in social situations	*kommunikative Fähigkeit/Kompetenz*
expert language	language that includes technical terms related to a specific subject	*Fachsprache*
four-letter words	swear/curse words	*Schimpfwort, Kraftausdruck*
Globish	a simplified form of international English	./.

lingua franca	a language chosen as a medium of communication used by people who speak different first languages	*Verkehrssprache, Lingua franca*
loan word/borrowing	a word from another language used in its original form	*Lehnwort*
mother tongue	the language that you first learn to speak when you are a child	*Muttersprache*
multilingual	with a command of several languages	*mehrsprachig*
native speaker	a speaker of a certain language as a first language	*Muttersprachler*
Netspeak	language varieties used to communicate on the Internet	*Netzjargon*
paraphrase	an alternative way of saying sth.	*Umschreibung*
phrase	a group of words that together have a particular meaning	*Wendung*
primary language	the language a person learned first, or the one he/she uses most often	*Primärsprache*
secondary language	a person's second language or one that is used less often	*Zweitsprache*
slang	informal, non-standard vocabulary	*Slang, Umgangssprache*
synonym	a word that has the same meaning as another word	*Synonym, sinnverwandtes Wort*

syntax	sentence structure	*Satzbau*
technical term	a word for a particular subject, that is difficult to understand if you do not know about that subject	*Fachbegriff*
texting	form of communication using the mobile phone shorthand	*SMS-Nachrichten schreiben oder verschicken*

English word/phrase	Explanation in English	German equivalent and/or synonym(s)
English		
AE/US *(abbr.)*	American English	*amerikanisches Englisch*
BE *(abbr.)*	British English	*britisches Englisch*
bisyllabic	consisting of two syllables	*zweisilbig*
Black English	variety of English spoken by African-Americans	*Afroamerikanisches Englisch*
dialect	a language variety with unique features of pronunciation, grammar and vocabulary used by speakers with a certain regional or social background	*Dialekt/Mundart*
Englishes	international varieties of English	*Varietäten des Englischen, z. B. Dialekt, Jugendsprache, Soziolekt etc.*
EFL *(abbr.)*	English as a Foreign Language	*Englisch als Fremdsprache*

ESL *(abbr.)*	English as a Second Language	*Englisch als Zweitsprache*
monosyllabic	consisting of a single syllable	*einsilbig*
non-standard English	informal or slang vocabulary, grammar or pronunciation	*nicht der sprachlichen Norm entsprechendes Englisch, z. B. Umgangssprache, Dialekt etc.*
official language	the language or one of the languages that is accepted by a country's government	*Amtssprache*
pronunciation	the way in which a language or a particular word or sound is pronounced	*Aussprache*
Queen's English	the 'prestige accent' known as Received Pronunciation	*englische Hochsprache*
RP [ˌɑː ˈpiː] *(abbr.)*	Received Pronunciation; the regionally neutral, prestige accent of British English	*britische Standardaussprache, anerkannte Aussprache*
spoken English	words and expressions mostly used in spoken English	*mündliche/ gesprochene Sprache*
standard English	a prestige variety of English, used as an institutionalized norm	*Standardenglisch*
syllable	an element of speech that acts as a unit of rhythm	*Silbe*

variety [vəˈraɪəti]	a situationally distinctive system of linguistic expression, e. g. formal, colloquial, etc.	*Abart, Spielart*
written English	words and expressions mostly used in written English	*Schriftsprache*

English word/phrase	Explanation in English	German equivalent and/or synonym(s)
linguistics		
capitalization	to begin a word with a capital letter	*Großschreibung*
collocation	when two or more words are often used together, e. g. fast food, a quick shower, to commit suicide, etc.	*Kollokation, gängige Wortverbindung*
consonant	a letter of the alphabet that represents a consonant sound	*Konsonant*
diphthong	a combination of two vowel sounds, e. g. the sounds [aɪ] in 'pipe'	*Doppellaut*
compound	a noun, an adjective or verb made of two or more words or joined by a hyphen. e. g. travel agent, dark-haired, etc.	*Wortverbindung*
linguistics	the science of language	*Sprachwissenschaft*

neologism	the creation of a new word	*Neologie, Neuschöpfung*
orthography [ɔː'θɒgrəfɪ]	spelling	*Rechtschreibung*
phonetics	the study of how humans make, transmit and receive speech sounds	*Phonetik, Lautschrift*
phonology	the study of the sound systems of languages	*Phonologie*
social variation	unique linguistic features that are related to the social background/class of speakers	*soziale Unterschiede*
terminology	the set of technical words or expressions used for a particular subject	*Fachsprache, Terminologie*
vowel	a letter that represents a vowel sound	*Vokal*

Do We Get What We Deserve? – Personal Identities and Social Relationships

English word/phrase	Explanation in English	German equivalent and/or synonym(s)
partnership • gender roles		
to achieve sth.	to successfully complete sth.	*etwas erreichen*
achievement	sth. important that you succeed in doing	*Errungenschaft/Ziel, das man erreicht hat*
convention	the way sth. is done that most people in a society expect and consider to be the right way	*Konvention; Gewohnheit*
emancipation	men and women having the same rights and opportunies	*Emanzipation; Gleichberechtigung*
femininity [ˌfeməˈnɪnəti]	qualities that are considered to be typical of women, esp. gentleness, delicateness and prettiness	*Weiblichkeit, Femininität*
to gain experience	to gradually get more and more knowledge and skills	*Erfahrung(en) sammeln*
gender roles	the position that men and women have in society	*Geschlechterrollen*
gender socialization [ˌsəʊʃəlaɪˈzeɪʃn]	the specific (and often different) way in which boys and girls are educated	*Geschlechtssozialisation*

to get through sth.	to come successfully to the end of a difficult time	*etwas hinter sich bringen*
legal emancipation	having the legal rights and responsibilities of an adult person	*rechtliche Gleichberechtigung*
to live up to sth.	to do what you were expected to do or what you promised to do	*einer Vorstellung entsprechen*
masculinity [ˌmæskjuˈlɪnəti]	qualities that are considered to be typical of men, esp. strength, muscularity, etc.	*Maskulinität, Männlichkeit*
quest (for) sth.	a long search for sth. that is difficult to find	*Suche/Streben nach etwas*
role model	sb. people admire and whose behaviour they try to copy	*Vorbild*
to search for one's own identity	the act of trying to find out who you are/ what your abilities/ qualities are	*seine Identität suchen; herausfinden, wer man ist*
socialization	the process by which sb., esp. a child, learns to behave in a socially acceptable way	*Sozialisation, Vergesellschaftung*
to team up with sb.	to join with sb. in order to work on sth.	*mit jdm. zusammenarbeiten*
transition	when sth. changes from one form to another	*Übergang, Wechsel*

English word/phrase	Explanation in English	German equivalent and/or synonym(s)
familiy • family ethics		
to acquire [ə'kwaɪə(r)] **basic skills**	to learn the most important things for life	*sich Grundkenntnisse aneignen*
baby hatch	a special facility that e. g. hospitals offer where newborn babies can be brought to if the mother does not want them or cannot take care of them	*Babyklappe*
blended family	a family in which parents have children from previous marriages	*eine Patchwork-Familie, mit Kindern aus vorherigen/verschiedenen Ehen/Beziehungen*
a close/close-knit family	a family whose members like/love each other very much	*enge Familienbande haben*
domestic quarrel	a quarrel within the family	*familiärer Streit*
extended family	a family that also includes grand-parents, aunts, etc.	*ausgedehnte (große) Familie*
family resemblance	similarity between members of a family, esp. in the way they look	*Familienähnlichkeit*
family values	traditional ideas about what a family should be like	*Familienwerte*
household chore [tʃɔː(r)]	a small job that you have to do regularly at home	*häusliche Pflicht*

marriage	the legal relationship between a husband and a wife	*Ehe*
nuclear family	a family that consists only of a wife, husband and children	*Kernfamilie (Vater, Mutter, Kind(er))*
to raise a child/ children	to look after children and help them grow	*to bring up; ein Kind/ Kinder großziehen*
same-sex marriage/ gay marriage	the marriage of two people of the same sex (man/man or woman/woman)	*gleichgeschlechtliche Ehe*
single-parent family	mother or father who looks after their children on their own, without a partner	*alleinerziehende Eltern*

English word/phrase	Explanation in English	German equivalent and/or synonym(s)
community		
accommodation	a place to live, work or stay	*Unterbringung*
affordable	cheap enough for people to buy or rent	*bezahlbar*
applicant	sb. who has formally asked, usually in writing, for a job	*Bewerber(in)*
to apply for sth.	to formally ask for sth., e. g. a job	*sich bewerben um*
to be at risk	to be in danger	*gefährdet sein*
built-up area	area/ground that is covered with buildings	*bebaute Fläche*
countryside	landscape	*Landschaft*

to demolish	to pull down a building	*abbrechen, abreißen*
to deteriorate	to become worse	*verwahrlosen, herunterkommen*
housing	houses, apartments, etc. that people live in	*Wohnraum*
housing shortage	not having enough houses, apartments	*Mangel an Wohnraum*
infrastructure	the basic organiza-tional structures needed for the operation of a society/enterprise	*Infrastruktur (z. B. Straßen, Wasserwege etc.)*
to meet sb.'s basic needs	to provide a situation in which people feel good and safe (e. g. enough water, food, housing, etc.)	*jemandes Grundbedürfnisse erfüllen*
municipal council	local administration	*Stadtverwaltung*
to pass legislation	to officially accept a law	*ein Gesetz verab-schieden*
(poor) sanitation	the public system of removing and treating waste or dirty water, etc.	*(unzureichende) sanitäre Anlagen*
population density	the amount of people that live in a particular place	*Bevölkerungsdichte*
to give preference to sb./sth.	to give sb./sth. better treatment or greater favour	*jdm./etwas den Vorzug geben*
to rehouse	to provide sb. with a different home to live in	*jdn. umsiedeln*
residency	the state of living in a particular place	*Anwohnerschaft*

residential area	area consisting of houses rather than factories, shops, etc.	*Wohngegend*
rural	connected with the countryside	*ländlich*
set of criteria	a set of standards that you use in order to make a decision	*Kriterienkatalog*
urban (area)	connected with a town or city	*städtisch*
urbanization	the process of turning countryside into cities	*Verstädterung*
urban growth	the growth of a city or town	*städtisches Wachstum*

English word/phrase	Explanation in English	German equivalent and/or synonym(s)
society • values		
accessible [ək'sesəbl]	able to be reached	*verfügbar, zugänglich*
to have access to sth.	to have the opportunity or right to use sth.	*Zugang zu etwas haben*
ageing	the process of becoming old	*das Altern; Älterwerden*
age group	a group of people of the same age	*Altersgruppe*
alienation	the feeling of not being part of a group	*Fremdheit*
to ban sth.	to prohibit or forbid sth.	*etwas verbieten*
civic duties	sth. you have to do because it is morally or legally right	*staatsbürgerliche Pflichten*

community-building	encouraging the feeling of sharing things or belonging to a group in the place where you live	*gemeinschaftsbildend*
community interests	interests of all people belonging to a community	*Gemeinschaftsinteresse*
(to make) demands on sth.	request for sth.	*an jdn. Forderungen stellen*
demography	the scientific study of the changing number of births, deaths, diseases, etc.	*Demografie; Bevölkerungswissen-schaft*
to demonstrate for one's rights	to fight for one's rights	*für seine Rechte demonstrieren/ eintreten*
demographic change	changes in population because of rising numbers of old people, fewer births, etc.	*demografischer Wandel*
discriminatory [dɪˈskrɪmɪnətəri]	treating sb. or a group of people worse than others in an unfair way	*diskriminierend*
discrimination of sb.	the practice of treating sb. or a particular group in society less fairly than others	*Diskriminierung von jmd.*
diversity [daɪˈvɜːsəti]	a range of different people, things or ideas	*Vielfalt*
(social) divide	social gap between different classes	*sozialer Unterschied/ Trennlinie*

the elderly	old people	*die ältere Generation, Senioren*
freedom of expression	the freedom to say or write what you think or feel	*Freiheit der Meinungsäußerung*
fundamentalism [ˌfʌndəˈmentəlɪzəm]	the practice of following very strictly the basic rules of any religion	*Fundamentalismus*
generation gap	the difference in attitude or behaviour between young and older people that causes lack of understanding	*Generationenkonflikt*
(gender) repression	the act of using force to control a group of people and restrict their freedom	*(Geschlechter-) Unterdrückung*
human needs	the things that sb. requires in order to live in a comfortable way	*menschliche Bedürfnisse*
internal (social) stability	the maintenance, constancy and reliability of social systems, e. g. patterns of relationships like family, work, business, etc.	*innere (soziale) Stabilität*
life expectancy	the number of years that a person is likely to live	*Lebenserwartung*
life-span	the length of time sb./sth. is likely to live	*Lebensdauer*
limitation	restriction	*Begrenzung, Einschränkung*

to meet sb.'s (basic) needs	to do or satisfy what is needed or sb. asks for	*jdms. Grundbedürfnisse erfüllen*
middle class	the social group between the upper and the working class	*Mittelschicht*
multiculturalism	the practice of giving importance to all cultures in a society	*Multikulturalismus*
old people's home/ nursing home	a residence, esp. one where old people live and are cared for	*Seniorenheim; Altenheim*
opinionated	having very strong opinions that you are not willing to change	*eigensinnig*
population	all the people who live in a particular area, city, country, etc.	*Bevölkerung*
population pyramid/ age structure	the age structure of a society or in a country	*Bevölkerungspyramide*
prejudice	an unreasonable dislike and distrust of people who are different from you in some way	*Vorurteil*
to be prejudiced	having an unreasonable dislike of or preference for sb./sth.	*voreingenommen sein*
privilege ['prɪvɪlɪdʒ]	a special right or advantage belonging to a particular person or group of people	*Privileg; Vorzug*
professional needs	requests related to work, e.g. fair and equal payment, satisfactory working conditions, etc.	*berufliche Bedürfnisse*

religious community	a group of people who have the same religion	*religiöse Gemeinschaft*
respect for sb./sth.	a feeling of admiration for sb./sth. because of their good qualities or achievements	*Respekt vor jmd./etw.*
to respect sb./sth.	to have a very good opinion of sb./sth.	*jmd./etw. respektieren*
senior citizen	an elderly/old person	*Senior(in); ältere(r) Bürger(in)*
social status	rank or position that sb. has in society	*sozialer Stand; soziale Position*
to stand out	to be easily seen; to be noticeable	*auffallen*
to undermine sth.	to make sth., esp. sb.'s confidence or authority, gradually weaker	*etwas untergraben*
upper class	the groups of people that are considered to have the highest social status and more money or power than other people in society	*Oberschicht*
welfare state	a state that provides practical or financial help to people or animals in need	*Wohlfahrtsstaat*
working-age people	people between 18 and 65 years	*Menschen im erwerbsfähigen Alter*

working class	the social class whose members do not have much money or power and are usually employed to do manual work	*Arbeiterklasse*

English word/phrase	Explanation in English	German equivalent and/or synonym(s)
human • professional needs and wants		
advancement	to get a financial raise; to get promoted	*Beförderung; sozialer Aufstieg*
aid/assistance	support	*Hilfe; Unterstützung*
antisocial	harmful or annoying to other people or society	*antisozial; unsozial*
basic human needs	basic requirements to live in dignity and comfort (e. g. food, love, shelter)	*menschliche Grundbedürfnisse*
contribution	a sum of money or action that helps support others in need	*Beitrag; Spende*
to deserve sth.	to have sth. because of what one is or has done	*etw. verdienen*
dignity	the state of being given honour and respect by people	*Würde*
disadvantaged	not having the things that others have; deprived	*benachteiligt*, deprived
discrimination	the practice of treating sb. less fairly than others	*Diskriminierung*

equality	the state of being equal in rights, status, advantages, etc.	*Gleichheit*
human rights	the basic rights that everyone has to be treated fairly and equally and not in a cruel way	*Menschenrechte*
share	a part of sth.	*Anteil; Beitrag*
shelter	a building that provides a place to stay e. g. for people without a home	*Asyl; Einrichtung für sozial Benachteiligte*
women's shelter	a building where women can stay when they are abused by their husbands or need help and advice	*Frauenhaus*

Learning for Life? Lifelong Learning? – Teaching, Learning and Education?

English word/phrase	Explanation in English	German equivalent and/or synonym(s)
education • learning		
admission/to admit sb.	to allow sb. to enter a place/an institution	*Zutritt, Zulassung/ hereinlassen, zulassen*
attendance (at sth.)	here: when students have to be present in lessons	*Anwesenheit*
to attend school	to go regularly to a school	*regelmäßig die Schule besuchen*
to be enrolled	to be officially registered at a school/university, etc.	*offiziell an einer Schule/Universität angemeldet/ eingeschrieben sein*
code of conduct	a set of rules or principles that tells students how to behave at school	*Schulordnung*
compulsory schooling	a particular number of years that children are required to go to school	*Schulpflicht*
curfew	the time, decided by a parent, by which the child must be at home in the evening	*Ausgangssperre, Ausgehverbot; hier: die Zeit, zu der Jugendliche (abends) zu Hause sein müssen*
to cut class *(infml.)*	to deliberately not go to a class	*Schule/Unterricht schwänzen*
diploma	a document showing that you have completed a course or a part of your education	*(Abschluss-) Diplom*

discipline	the ability to control your own behaviour (so that you do what you are expected to do)	*Disziplin*
to drop out of school	to leave school without a diploma	*die Schule ohne Abschluss verlassen*
enrolment	the process of registering at/for a school/university/course, etc.	*Anmeldung, Einschreibung*
entrance exam	exam taken to get the permission to attend a certain school, university, etc.	*Zulassungsprüfung*
extra-curricular activity	activity that is not part of the usual studies	*Aktivität außerhalb des Stundenplans*
fee	an amount of money that you pay, e. g. to go to a certain school	*Gebühr, Schulgeld*
to fund sth.	to provide money for sth./sb.	*etwas finanzieren*
graduate	a person who has completed his school studies	*(Schul-/Hochschul-) Absolvent*
high school diploma	a document showing that you have completed high school	*Oberschulabschluss*
grade	a mark given in an exam; one of the levels in school	*Schulnote; Jahrgang*
to graduate from high school	to complete high school with a diploma	*die Schule erfolgreich (mit einem Abschluss) abschließen*

graduation	the act of successfully finishing school/ college/university, etc.	*(Schul-/Studien-) Abschluss*
optional (subject)	sth. that you can choose	*Wahlfach*
to pay tuition fees	to pay money to be taught, e. g. at university or college	*Studiengebühr(en) bezahlen*
to play truant ['truːənt]	to stay away from school without permission	*die Schule/den Unterricht schwänzen*
proficient [prə'fɪʃnt]**/ proficiency**	to be able to do sth. well because of training and practice	*tüchtig, kenntnisreich/ Können, Kenntnisse*
report	a written statement by teachers about a child's work at school	*Zeugnis*
SAT (Scholastic Assessment Test)	a test taken in the U.S. by high school students who want to go to college or university	*Zulassungstest, Eignungstest*
scholarship	an amount of money that is given to sb. by an educational organization to help pay for their educa-tion	*Stipendium*
to pass an exam	to achieve the required exam standard; opp.: fail	*eine Prüfung bestehen*
to take a course/ an exam	to study a particular subject/to participate in an exam	*an einem Kurs/einer Prüfung teilnehmen*
truancy ['truːənsi]	the act of staying away from school without permission	*das Schwänzen von Schule/Unterricht*

English word/phrase	Explanation in English	German equivalent and/or synonym(s)
school systems		
advanced	at a high or difficult level or at a late stage of development	*fortgeschritten*
A-levels	an examination that students take usually when they are 18 (advanced level)	*Abitur*
art	the subjects you can study at school or university that are not scientific	*Kunst*
assessment test	a test made to find out what the students' weaknesses and strengths are	*Lernerfolgs-/ Leistungstest*
college (BE)	a place where students go to study or receive training after they have left school	*Fachhochschule*
college (AE)	a university where students can study for a degree after they have left school	*Universität mit Bachelor-Abschluss*
comprehensive school	a secondary school for young people of all levels of ability	*Gesamtschule*
compulsory subject	a subject that students have to take	*Pflichtfach*
computer science	a study of computers and how they can be used	*Informatik*

curriculum	the subjects that are included in a course of study or taught in a school, college, etc.	*Lehrplan*
elementary education	the education, teaching, etc. of children normally between 6 and 11/12	*grundlegende Schulbildung*
elementary school (US)	a school for children between the ages of 6 and 12	*Grundschule*
engineering	the study of design, building and control of machines	*Technik und Konstruktion*
faculty (AE)	the people who work at a school, college or university	*Lehrerkollegium*
GCSE *(abbr.)*	General Certificate of Secondary Education	*mittlerer Schulabschluss in Großbritannien*
grade (AE)	one of the levels in a school with children of the same age	*Schulklasse*
health education	subject connected with the condition of a person's body and mind	*Gesundheitserziehung/-lehre*
higher education	education and training at a university or college	*Hochschulausbildung, akademische Ausbildung*
high school (US)	school for young people between the ages of 14 and 18	*Sekundarschule; Oberschule*
home economics	cooking and other skills needed at home, taught as a subject at school	*Hauswirtschaftslehre*

intermediate	having more than a basic knowledge of sth. but not yet advanced	*Mittelstufe*
kindergarten	a school or class to prepare children aged 5 for school	*Kindergarten*
mathematics	the subject connected with the science of numbers and shapes	*Mathematik*
NVQ [ˌen viː ˈkjuː] *(abbr.)*	National Vocational Qualification	*Fachabitur*
nursery school	early education for children between 2 and 5	*Kindergarten*
physical education (PE)	sport and exercise that is taught in schools	*Sportunterricht*
primary education	the education of children between 5 and 11 years	*Grundschule*
required subject	a subject that students have to take	*Pflichtfach*
science	a subject connected with the study of the structure and behaviour of the natural world	*Naturwissenschaften*
secondary education	the education, teaching, etc. of children between the ages of 11 and 16 or 18	*weiterführende Schule/ Ausbildung; Sekundarstufe II*
social studies	a subject connected with the study of people and society	*Sozialwissenschaften*

staff (BE)	the people who work at a school, college or university	*Lehrerkollegium*
stage	a period or state sb./sth. passes through while developing or making progress	*Stufe*
timetable/schedule	a list showing particular times at which events/lessons take place	*Stundenplan*
vocational school	a school that teaches or relates to the skills you need to do a particular job	*Berufsschule*
year (BE)		*Schuljahr, Klassenstufe*

English word/phrase	Explanation in English	German equivalent and/or synonym(s)
	lifelong learning	
to acquire [ə'kwaɪər] **basic skills**	to learn the most important things for life	*sich Grundkenntnisse aneignen*
to add to one's knowledge	to learn sth. new	*sich neue Kenntnisse aneignen*
after-school tutoring	getting private lessons from a teacher after school	*Hausaufgabenbetreu-ung, Privatunterricht/Nachhilfe*
computer literacy	ability to handle a computer	*mit einem Computer umgehen können*
literacy	the ability to read and write	*die Lese- und Schreibfähigkeit*
to be illiterate	not being able to read and write	*ein Analphabet sein*
to be literate	being able to read and write	*lesen und schreiben können*

to mentor sb.	to help and advise a person with less experience	*jdn. betreuen/beraten*
qualification(s)	a skill or type of experience that you need for a particular job	*Qualifikation, Fähigkeit(en)*
to retrain	to learn a new type of work/a new skill	*umschulen*
(un)skilled	(not) having special training/qualifications	*(un-)gelernt, (un-) ausgebildet*
semi-skilled	having some special training/qualifications but less than skilled people	*angelernt (d. h. mit Berufskenntnissen, aber ohne Abschluss)*
placement	a job, usually as part of a course or study, which gives you experience of a particular type of work	*Praktikantenstelle*
vocational training	training connected with a job	*Berufsschulausbildung*

English word/phrase	Explanation in English	German equivalent and/or synonym(s)
health education • nutrition • anorexia • obesity		
anorexia	mental illness that makes sb. avoid eating	*Magersucht*
anorexic	suffering from anorexia	*magersüchtig sein*
appearance	the way sb. looks to other people	*(äußere) Erscheinung*
(physical) attractive-ness	the quality of being good looking	*Attraktivität, gutes Aussehen*

to be a particular weight	how heavy sb. is	*ein bestimmtes Gewicht haben*
big	when sb. has a large body	*schwer, dick*
to binge on sth.	to eat or drink too much, esp. without being able to control yourself	*übermäßig essen oder trinken*
AIDS *(abbr.)*	acquired immune deficiency syndrome (an illness which attacks the body's ability to resist infection and which usually causes death)	*AIDS*
BMI (body mass index)	the relationship between your height and your weight	*das Verhältnis zwischen Körpergröße und Gewicht*
body weight	how heavy your body is	*Körpergewicht*
to border on obsession	sth. very unhealthy that you cannot control or that almost gets out of control	*an Besessenheit grenzen*
bulimia [buːˈlɪmiə]	an illness in which a person cannot stop eating too much, and then vomits in order to control their weight	*Ess-Brechsucht, Bulimie*
chubby	slightly fat in a nice-looking way (babies)	*pummelig*
diet	the food that you eat and drink regularly	*Ernährung*

eating disorder	mental condition in which you do not eat a normal amount of food	*Essstörung*
eating habit(s)	the practice of what or how sb. eats	*Essgewohnheiten*
fat	weighing too much	*übergewichtig*
fat intake	the amount of fat you eat	*das Zusichnehmen von Fett*
to gain/lose weight	to increase/decrease how heavy you are	*zunehmen/abnehmen*
to get/keep your weight down	to lose weight	*sein Gewicht reduzieren*
good-looking	attractive	*gutaussehend, attraktiv*
handsome	good-looking (man)	*gutaussehend, attraktiv*
HIV [ˌeɪtʃ aɪ ˈviː] *(abbr.)*	human immunodeficiency virus (the virus that can cause AIDS)	*HIV-Erkrankung*
sb.'s ideal weight	the weight that is healthy and best for sb.	*Idealgewicht*
image (of sb.)	a picture that you have in your mind, esp. about what sb./sth. is like or the way they look	*(geistige) Vorstellung von jdm./etwas haben*
nutrition	the process by which living things receive the food necessary for them to grow and be healthy	*Ernährung*
obese [əʊˈbiːs]	extremely fat in a way that is dangerous to your health	*fettleibig*

obesity	when sb. is very fat in a way that is unhealthy	*Fettleibigkeit, extremes Übergewicht*
overweight	weighing more than you should	*übergewichtig*
plus-size	euphemistic for fat or obese	*Übergröße*
promiscuity [ˌprɒmɪsˈkjuːəti]	the situation of having many sexual partners	*wechselnde sexuelle Partner haben*
role model	sb. whose behaviour, attitudes, etc. people try to copy because they admire them	*Idol*
(to practise) safe sex	to use condoms in order to prevent the transmission of sexual diseases	*sicheren Geschlechtsverkehr praktizieren, z. B. indem man Kondome benutzt*
(to have) sexual intercourse	to have sex with sb.	*Geschlechtsverkehr (haben)*
skinny	very thin	*mager*
slim	attractively thin	*schlank;* slender
to starve oneself	to eat very little food in order to become thinner	*(sich schlank) hungern*
STD (sexually transmitted disease)	diseases that are transmitted by having sex	*Geschlechtskrankheit*
tall	a person that is of more than average height	*groß, lang*
underweight	weighing less than is expected or usual	*untergewichtig*

to watch your weight	to be careful (e.g. by eating not too much) in order not to gain any weight	*auf sein Gewicht achten*
well-being	feeling of being happy and healthy	*Wohlgefühl*
well-built	sb. who is well-built has a big, strong body	*gut gebaut*

A World on the Move: Global Migration and Mobility

English word/phrase	Explanation in English	German equivalent and/or synonym(s)
	minorities • multiculturalism	
alien ['eɪliən]	a person who is not a citizen of the country in which they live and work	*Fremde/r*
anti-discrimination legislation	laws against discrimination	*Gesetzgebung gegen Diskriminierung/ ungerechte Behandlung*
to assimilate/ assimilation	to become a part of a country/community	*sich anpassen/ Anpassung*
census	the process of officially counting a country's population	*Volkszählung*
to conform to sth.	to obey a rule, to agree with	*sich (einer Meinung/ einem Vorschlag etc.) anschließen*
to contribute to sth.	to give sth. or help sb.	*zu etwas beitragen, helfen*
to decline	to become smaller, fewer, weaker	*weniger werden, abnehmen (in Menge);* *to decrease*
descendant	a person's descendants are their children, their children's children and all persons who live after them who are related to them	*Nachkomme;* relative
to discriminate against sb.	to treat one person worse/better than another in an unfair way	*jdn. unfair behandeln, diskrimieneren*
diversity ['daɪ'vɜːsɪti]	variety	*Vielfalt*

equality	the state of being equal in rights, status, advantages, etc.	*Gleichheit (gleiche Rechte haben), gleichberechtigt sein*
ethnic/ethnicity	connected with a nation, race or people that shares certain cultural traditions	*Volks-; Volkszugehörigkeit*
foreign-born	born in a different country from the one you live in	*im Ausland geboren, ausländischer Herkunft*
(cultural/ethnic) heritage	the history and traditions that a country has had for many years and that have become an important part of its character	*(kulturelles/völkisches) Erbe*
Hispanic	a person whose first language is Spanish, esp. one who comes from a Latin-American country	*Lateinamerikaner(in), Südamerikaner(in)*
to integrate sb./ integration	to enable sb. to become accepted as a member of a social group	*jdn. miteinbeziehen, integrieren; Integration*
(cultural) interaction	the act of communicating with sb. (from a different culture)	*gegenseitige (kulturelle) Einwirkung*
interracial	involving people of different races	*zwischen (den) verschiedenen Rassen*
to live on charity	to live on money/ food/help that organizations or other people give/donate to sb.	*von Almosen leben*

multi-ethnic	involving or including several different races	*Vielvölker-*
population	all the people who live in a particular area, city or country	*Bevölkerung*
refugee ['refju'dʒi]	someone who has been forced to leave a country, especially during a war, or for political or religious reasons	*Flüchtling*
resident	someone who lives or stays in a particular place	*Anwohner*
to settle (in a place)	to go to live in a new place, and stay there for a long time	*sich eingewöhnen/ niederlassen (in/an einen/einem Ort)*
temporary stay	a stay continuing for only a limited period of time	*befristeter Aufenthalt*
Western values	the beliefs, traditions, customs etc. of the Western community	*westliche Werte*

English word/phrase	Explanation in English	German equivalent and/or synonym(s)
	migration • immigration policy	
asylum seeker [ə'saɪləm]	a person who has been forced to leave their own country to escape danger and who, after arriving in another country, asks to be allowed to stay there	*Asylant(in)*
to apply for (a visa)	to make a formal request for sth.	*einen Antrag stellen auf*

application	a formal request for sth.	*Antrag*
border/boundary	the line that divides two areas or countries	*Grenze*
border control	measures taken to prevent illegal immigrants from entering a country	*Grenzkontrolle*
citizen(ship)	a person who has the legal right to belong to a particular country	*Staatsbürger(schaft)*
cultural clash	multiculturalism	*Zusammenprall der Kulturen*
to deport sb.	to force sb. to leave a country	*jdn. abschieben*
destination	a place that sb. is going or being sent to	*Bestimmungsort, Ziel*
economic migrant ['maɪgrənt]	a person who has left their homeland because the economic situation there is very bad	*Wirtschaftsflüchtling*
to emigrate (from)	to leave one's own country in order to live in another	*auswandern*
emigration	the process of leaving one's own country in order to live in another	*Emigration, Auswanderung*
to expel sb. [ɪk'spel]	to force sb. to leave a country	*jdn. ausweisen*
illegal alien	an illegal immigrant	*illegaler Einwanderer*
to immigrate (to) ['ɪmɪgreɪt]	to come into a country in order to live there permanently	*immigrieren, einwandern*

immigration control	the place where the passports and other documents of the people coming into the country are checked	*Einwanderungskon-trolle*
to go through immigration	to pass the immigra-tion control	*die Einwanderungskon-trolle/Passkontrolle etc. durchlaufen*
to immerse in a culture	to adopt the customs and beliefs of a culture; to adjust to a culture	*eintauchen, einfließen*
immigration policy	the way a government deals with the immigration of people to its country	*Einwanderungspolitik*
to integrate, integration	to become part of a group or society and be accepted by them, or to help someone do this	*integrieren, Integration*
interracial marriage	marriage between different races of people	*gemischtrassige Ehe*
(cultural) interaction	the act of communi-cating with sb. (from a different culture)	*(kulturelle) Interaktion*
legal/illegal immi-grant	a person who according to the law is (not) allowed to permanently live in a country after leaving his/her own country	*legaler/illegaler Einwanderer*
migrant	a person who moves from one place to another, esp. to find work	*Gastarbeiter(in); Wanderarbeiter(in)*

migration	the movement of large numbers of people from one place to another	*(Ab-)Wanderung (von Menschen)*
naturalization	to become a citizen of a particular country	*Einbürgerung*
out of economic necessity	for economic reasons	*wegen wirtschaftlicher Notwendigkeiten/ Zwänge*
to persecute sb.	to treat sb. in an unfair and cruel way because of their race, gender, religion or political beliefs	*jdn. verfolgen*
persecution	the act of hunting down or treating sb. in an unfair and cruel way because of their race, gender, religion or beliefs	*Verfolgung*
quota system	a system that allows only a limited number of people to immi-grate	*Quotensystem*
to take an oath of allegiance [ə'liːdʒəns]	to make a formal and very serious promise of loyalty	*den Treueeid schwören*

English word/phrase	Explanation in English	German equivalent and/or synonym(s)
colonization • historical development		
(colonial) policy	a way of doing sth. that has been officially agreed and chosen by a political party	*Kolonialpolitik; Politik/ Vorgehensweise, auf die sich Kolonialmächte geeinigt haben*

colonial power	a country that controls another country	*Kolonialmacht*
to colonize	to establish political control over another country, and send your citizens there to settle	*kolonialisieren*
colonization [ˌkɒlənaɪˈzeɪʃn]	the act of establishing political control over another country and sending your citizens there to settle	*Kolonialisierung*
colony	a country that is under the political control of a more powerful country, usually one that is far away	*Kolonie*
colonist	sb. who settles in a new colony	*Kolonist, Bewohner einer Kolonie*
to conquer [ˈkɒŋkə(r)]	to get control of a country by fighting	*erobern*
conqueror	a person (often an army) who fights to get control of a country	*Eroberer*
to decolonize sb.	to make a former colony politically independent	*entkolonialisieren, die Kolonialisierung rückgängig machen/ aufheben*
to discover	if sb. discovers a new place, they are the first persons to find it	*entdecken*
to divide sth. up	to separate sth. into parts and share them between people	*etwas aufteilen*

to expand	to become larger in size, number or account	*vergrößern, ausdehnen;* to increase
to explore	to look for sth. such as land, minerals, gold, etc.	*erforschen, erkunden*
exploration	the act of travelling through a place in order to find out about it	*Erforschung, Erkundung*
to invade	to enter a country using military force in order to take control of it	*einmarschieren, überfallen;* to occupy
invasion [ɪn'veɪʒn]	the act of invading a country	*Einmarsch, Überfall;* occupation
native	a person who was born in a particular country	*Ureinwohner*
postcolonial	later than or after colonialism	*nach der Kolonialzeit*
raw [rɔː] **materials**	natural substances that are used in manufacturing goods	*Rohstoffe*
resources [rɪ'sɔːsɪz]	soil, minerals, forests, water and energy sources	*Ressourcen, z. B. Rohstoffe, Boden etc.*
to reign	to rule a nation as their king, queen or emperor	*regieren, herrschen*
rule	to have the official power to control a country	*Herrschaft*
to settle/settlement	to make a place/a country your permanent home	*(be-)siedeln; Besiedlung*

English word/phrase	Explanation in English	German equivalent and/or synonym(s)
beliefs • values • dreams of success		
authority [ɔːθɒrəti]	the power you have because of your official position	*Autorität, Amtsgewalt*
cultural patterns/ habits	cultural ideas/ behaviour	*kulturelle Muster/ Gewohnheiten*
to be equal to sb./sth.	to have the same rights as sb./sth.	*gleichberechtigt sein*
from rags to riches	becoming very rich after starting life very poor	*vom Tellerwäscher zum Millionär*
God's chosen people	a small number of people having been selected by God for a special relationship with him	*Gottes auserwähltes Volk*
heterogenous society [ˌhetərəˈdʒiːniəs]	a very diverse society	*verschiedenartige, breit gefächerte Gesellschaft*
to identify with sb./ sth.	to feel sympathy for sb./sth. or be able to share their feelings	*sich mit jmd./etw. identifizieren*
identification [aɪˌdentɪfɪˈkeɪʃn]	a strong feeling of sympathy and similarity with someone	*Identifikation*
inalienable/unalien-able rights [ɪnˈeɪlɪənəbl]	rights that cannot be taken from you	*unveräußerlich*
individuality [ˌɪndɪˌvɪdʒuˈæləti]	the qualities that make someone or sth. different from other things or people	*Individualität*

melting pot	a place where people from different races, cultures etc live together	*Schmelztiegel (der Kulturen)*
national anthem	the official song of a nation that is sung or played on public occasions	*Nationalhymne*
national pride	being proud of having a particular nationality	*Nationalstolz*
to offer an opportunity to sb.	to give sb. a chance to do sth.	*jdm. eine Gelegenheit bieten*
patriotism ['peɪtriətɪzəm]	when you love your country and are proud of it	*Patriotismus*
(to be) patriotic	having or expressing a great love of your country	*patriotisch (sein)*
prosperity	wealth	*Reichtum, Wohlstand*
pursuit of happiness [pə'sjuːt]	when someone tries constantly to achieve happiness	*Streben nach Glück, existentieller Sicherheit, Zufriedenheit*
religious tolerance [rɪ'lɪdʒəs 'tɒlərəns]	no discrimination of people from different religions and beliefs	*religiöse Toleranz*
self-improvement	the process of trying to become a better and happier person	*(selbstständige) Weiterbildung*
a set of ideas/values	a group of ...	*Ideen-/Werteansammlung*
unlimited/limitless possibilities	endless opportunities and possibilities	*unbegrenzte/begrenzte Möglichkeiten*

English word/phrase	Explanation in English	German equivalent and/or synonym(s)
	economy	
bankruptcy	the state of being unable to pay your debts	*Pleite*
to go bankrupt	to become officially unable to pay your debts	*Pleite gehen;* to go bust
capacity for sth. [k'əpæsəti]	the amount of space for sth.	*Kapazität für etwas*
capitalism ['kæpɪtəlɪzəm]	an economic and political system in which businesses belong mostly to private owners, not to the government	*Kapitalismus*
to drop	to fall to a lower level or amount	*fallen, einbrechen*
financial recession	a difficult time when there is less business activity, trade, etc. in a country	*finanzielle Rezession, Flaute*
hire and fire policy	to employ and dismiss people in quick succession	*Einstellen und Feuern von Beschäftigten*
to be low-income	to be below an acceptable or usual level or quality of income	*geringverdienend sein*
real estate ['riːəl ɪ'steɪt] *(US)*	property in the form of land and houses	*Grundbesitz*
to subsidize ['sʌbsɪdaɪz]	if a government subsidizes a company, activity etc, it pays parts of its costs	*subventionieren*

subsidy ['sʌbsədi]	money that is paid by a government or organization to make prices lower and reduce the cost of producing goods	*Subvention*
to tax sb.	to make sb. pay an amount of money to the government according to their income, property etc	*jdn./etwas besteuern*
tax system	the system of charging taxes	*Steuersystem*
upward mobility	the act of moving up through the social classes and becoming richer	*sozialer Aufstieg*
wealth [welθ]	a large amount of money etc that a person or country owns	*Wohlstand;* prosperity
to be wealthy	to have a lot of property, money etc	*wohlhabend sein;* prosperous

Technology and Society: Steam, Steel and Science

English word/phrase	Explanation in English	German equivalent and/or synonym(s)
	science & technology	
to address sth.	to deal with a certain topic	*thematisieren*
artificial intelligence	the study of how to make computers do intelligent things that people can do	*künstliche Intelligenz*
breakthrough	an important development that may lead to an agreement or achievement	*Durchbruch*
computing	the act/activity of using computers; to work with computers	*mit dem Computer arbeiten/umgehen*
to develop sth.	to think of or produce a new product	*entwickeln;* to design
digital (lifestyle)	way of life that is fundamentally influenced by the electronic media, e. g. computers, the Internet, etc.	*digitaler Lebensstil*
efficient	doing sth. well and thoroughly with no waste of time or money or energy	*effizient, wirksam*
exploration	an examination of sth. in order to find out about it	*Erforschung*

to explore	to examine sth. completely or carefully in order to find out more about it	*erforschen*
to generate sth.	to produce or create sth.	*erzeugen, erzielen*
the Industrial Revolution	a period from 1750–1850 where changes in agriculture, manufacturing, mining, transportation and technology had profound effects on the economic, social and cultural conditions; James Watt's steam engine (ca. 1770) propelled the development in Great Britain and the world	*die industrielle Revolution*
to invent sth.	to make, design, or think of a new type of thing	*etwas erfinden*
invention	a useful machine, tool, instrument, etc. that has been invented	*Erfindung*
inventor	a person, who has invented sth. or whose job is to invent things	*Erfinder, Entwickler*
(instruction) manual	detailed information on how to do or use sth., e.g. a brochure or booklet	*Gebrauchsanleitung/ -anweisung*
manufacturing	the business or industry of producing goods in factories	*Herstellung*

microelectronics [ˌmaɪkrəʊ ɪˌlek'trɒnɪks]	the design, production and use of very small electronic circuits, that are used in computers	*Mikroelektronik*
progress	the process of improving or developing, or of getting closer to finishing or achieving something	*Fortschritt*
progressive	in favour of new or modern ideas, methods, and change	*fortschrittlich*
research	the careful study of a subject	*Forschung, Recherche*
researcher	sb. who studies a subject in detail in order to discover new information	*Forscher*
robot ['rəʊbɒt]	a machine that can perform a complicated series of tasks automatically	*Roboter*
robotics [rəʊ'bɒtiks]	the science of operating and designing robots	*Robotertechnik*
scientist ['saɪəntɪst]	an expert who studies or works in one or more of the sciences	*Wissenschaftler*
scientific (research)	involving or connected with science	*wissenschaftlich (-e Forschung)*

steam engine	a heat engine (external combustion engine) that performs mechanical work using steam as its working fluid; improved by Scottish inventor James Watt (ca. 1770) the machine fundamentally started the Industrial Revolution in England	*Dampfmaschine*
(to keep sb. under) surveillance [sɜːˈveɪləns]	the act of carefully watching a person suspected of a crime or a place where a crime may be committed	*Überwachung;* observation
technical instruction	detailed information on how to do or use sth.	*(technische) Gebrauchsanleitung;* directions
technological progress	progress which is relating to or involving technology	*technologischer Fortschritt*

English word/phrase	Explanation in English	German equivalent and/or synonym(s)
	genetic engineering	
advance	progress	*Fortschritt*
cloning	the act of producing a plant or an animal artificially from the cells of another plant or animal and thus producing sth. identical	*Klonen*

controversial	causing a lot of angry public discussion and disagreement	*kontrovers, umstritten*
to cross species	to mix two different kinds of animal breed or plant seed together	*Gattungen/Arten kreuzen*
to decode sth.	to discover the meaning of sth., especially sth. that has been written in a code	*etw. entschlüsseln*
to determine sth.	to discover the facts about sth.	*etw. bestimmen*
DNA	the chemical in the cells of all living things that carries genetic information	*DNA*
DNA fingerprinting	genetic fingerprinting	*genetischer Finger-abdruck*
embryonic stem cell	a basic type of cell in the body of an embryo, which can divide and develop into cells with particular functions	*Embryonenstamm-zellen*
a question of ethics	a question that deals with moral principles	*eine Frage der Ethik*
ethical concern	a concern that is connected with beliefs and principles about what is right and wrong	*ethisches Bedenken*
gene [dʒiːn]	a unit inside a cell which controls a particular quality in a living thing	*Gen*

genetics [dʒə'netɪks]	the study of how the qualities of living things are passed on in their genes	*Genetik*
genetic disorder	genetic defect	*genetischer Defekt*
genetic engineering	the science of changing the information in a living being's genes	*Gentechnik*
genome	the complete set of genes in a cell or living thing	*Genom*
GM food	genetically modified food	*gentechnisch veränderte Lebensmittel*
herbicide resistant	not damaged or affected by chemical substances used to kill unwanted plants	*resistent gegen Unkrautvernichtungsmittel*
to implant sth. into	to put sth. into a part of the body for medical purposes	*etw. implantieren*
to insert sth. into	to put sth. into sth. else or between two things	*etw. einfügen*
in vitro fertilization [ˌfɜːtəlaɪ'zeiʃn]	the process by which eggs are fertilized outside the body	*künstliche Befruchtung außerhalb des Körpers*
laboratory [lə'bɒrətri]	a room or buildung used for scientific research, experiments or testing	*Labor*
to manipulate [mə'nɪpjuleɪt]	to control or influence sb./sth., often in a dishonest way	*manipulieren*

to map sth.	to discover or give information about sth., especially the way it is arranged or organized	*etw. erfassen*
to modify sth. genetically	to change the genetic code of sth.	*den genetischen Code verändern*
reproductive technology	technology connected with reproducing babies, young animals, plants	*Reproduktionstech-nologie*
sample	a small amount of a substance taken from a larger amount in order to test it	*Muster, Probe*
to screen sb. for a disease	to examine sb. in order to find out if they have a particular disease	*jdn. auf eine Krankheit untersuchen*
sequence ['siːkwəns]	a set of related things which have a particular order	*Sequenz, Abfolge*
therapeutic [ˌθerə'pjuːtɪk]	designed to help treat an illness	*therapeutisch*

English word/phrase	Explanation in English	German equivalent and/or synonym(s)
	utopia • dystopia	
allegory ['æləgəri]	a fictional text which has both a literal and figurative meaning	*Gleichnis, Allegorie*
allegorical [ˌæləgɒrɪkl]	a story, painting, etc. in which the events and characters represent ideas or teach a moral lesson	*sinnbildlich*

anti-utopia	a futuristic world in which individual freedom is severely limited	*Antiutopie, Dystopie*
anti-utopian	connected with anti-utopias	*antiutopisch, dystopisch*
apocalyptic literature	literature which deals with the end of the world	*apokalyptische Literatur, Endzeit-Literatur*
authoritarian state [ɔːˌθɒrɪ'teəriən steɪt]	a state in which people are forced to obey authority and rules, even when these are wrong and unfair	*autoritärer Staat*
to be doomed	to be certain to fail or suffer	*verdammt sein*
doom	death or destruction	*Untergang, Verderben*
dystopia	a failed or fallen society	*Dystopie*
dystopian [dɪs'təʊpiən]	related to an imaginary state or place in which everything is extremely bad or unpleasant	*dystopisch*
to envision	to imagine	*sich ausmalen, sich vorstellen*
fictitious	invented by a writer	*fiktiv*
futuristic	extremely modern and unusual in appearance, as if belonging to a future time	*futuristisch*

hierarchy [ˈhaɪərɑːki]	a system in a society or an organization, in which people are organized into different levels of importance	*Hierarchie, Rangordnung*
hierarchical [ˌhaɪəˈrɑːkɪkl]	arranged in a hierarchy	*hierarchisch*
ideal society	a society without fault, a perfect society	*ideale Gesellschaft*
imaginary [ɪˈmædʒɪnəri]	existing only in your mind or imagination	*imaginär, erfunden, eingebildet*
narrative fiction	books and stories about imaginary people and events	*erzählende Literatur*
nightmare	a dream that is very frightening or unpleasant	*Albtraum*
nightmarish	frightening, horrific	*albtraumhaft, beklemmend*
oppression of people	the act of treating people unfairly or cruelly and preventing them from having opportunities and freedom	*Unterdrückung v. Menschen*
science fiction	science fantasy, scientific or technological speculation	*Science-Fiction*
snooper state	*(infml.)* a state that tries to find out private things about people	*Schnüffelstaat*

totalitarian state [təʊˌtælə'teəriən steɪt]	a state in which there is only one political party that has complete power and control over the people	*totalitärer Staat*
surveillance [sɜː'veɪləns]	the act of carefully watching a person or a place because they may be connected with crime	*Überwachung*
utopia [juː'təʊpiə]	an imaginary place or state in which everything is perfect	*Utopie*
utopian *(adj.)*	idealistic	*utopisch*
visionary ['vɪʒənri]	with the ability to imagine how a country, etc. will develop in the future	*visionär*

English word/phrase	Explanation in English	German equivalent and/or synonym(s)
	trade	
(to take) advantage of sb./sth.	(to make use of) an opportunity	*eine Gelegenheit (ausnutzen);* to exploit
to benefit from sth.	to profit from sth.	*von etw. profitieren*
benefit	advantage	*Vorteil, Nutzen*
commerce	trade	*Handel*
economic power	the state of having a lot of influence because of being able to produce, buy, or sell a lot	*Wirtschaftskraft*

(economic) suprema-cy [suːˈpreməsi]	a position in which you have more power, authority or status than anyone else	*Übermacht, Überlegenheit*
to exploit sb./sth.	to treat a person or situation as an opportunity to gain an advantage for yourself; to develop or use sth. for business or industry	*jdn./etw. ausnutzen/ ausbeuten*
exploitation of sb./ sth.	a situation in which sb. treats sb. else in an unfair way, esp. in order to make money from their work; the use of land, oil, minerals, etc.	*Ausnutzung/ Ausbeutung*
industrialized country	a country which has many industries	*Industriestaat/-nation*
to manufacture sth.	to produce sth.	*herstellen, produzieren*
to provide sth.	to make sth. available	*zur Verfügung stellen*
raw [rɔː] **materials**	natural substances that are used in manufacturing goods	*Rohstoffe, Rohmaterial*
resources [rɪˈsɔːsəz]	soil, minerals, forests, water and energy sources	*Ressourcen*
to run sth. for profit	to do sth. because you want to make money with it	*etw. für Profit/aus Profitgründen tun*
secure markets	safe markets	*sichere Märkte*
sweatshop	a place where people work for low wages in poor conditions	*Ausbeutungsbetrieb*

to trade with	to buy and sell goods as your business	*handeln mit*
trading post/trading station	a place where people can buy and exchange goods in a country	*Handelsstation, Handelsposten*
trading company	a business that buys and sells goods, esp. internationally	*Handelsgesellschaft*
transatlantic trade	trade/business involving countries on both sides of the Atlantic	*transatlantischer Handel*
transportation network	a system of roads/canals/railroads to transport goods	*Verkehrsnetz, Transportnetzwerk*
triangular trade	trade involving three continents: Europe, Africa and America	*Dreieckshandel*
wealth [welθ]	a large amount of money, property or valuable possessions that a person or a country owns	*Reichtum*

Technological Progress and Responsibility – (Green) Technology to Save the World?

English word/phrase	Explanation in English	German equivalent and/or synonym(s)
	environment	
biodegradable [ˌbaɪəʊdɪ'greidəbl]	changing a substance into a harmless natural state by using bacteria	*kompostierbar*
crude oil	oil that is in its natural condition before it is made pure or separated into different products	*Rohöl*
to decompose	to rot	*verrotten, kompostieren*
deforestation	cutting or burning down trees, forests	*Abholzung/Rodung von Wald*
to dispose of sth.	to get rid of sth.	*sich einer Sache entledigen*
environmentally-friendly	not harmful to the environment	*umweltfreundlich*
environmental safeguard	institution that helps protect the environment from damage	*Umweltschutzeinrichtung*
fossil fuel	fuel such as coal or oil, formed over millions of years from the remains of animals or plants	*fossile Brennstoffe (z. B. Öl, Kohle)*
greenhouse effect	the problem of the gradual rise in temperature in the air surrounding the Earth → global warming	*globale Erderwärmung*

habitat	the natural home of a plant or animal	*Lebensraum*
to incinerate	to burn sth.	*etwas verbrennen*
to intensify sth.	to heighten	*etwas verstärken, intensivieren*
(ir-)reversible	sth. that can(not) be changed back	*(nicht) umkehrbar*
organic farming	farming without using chemicals	*organische Landwirtschaft*
ozone layer	a layer of gases in the sky that prevents harmful radiation from the sun reaching the Earth	*Ozonschicht*
power station	large plant where electricity is produced	*Kraftwerk*
to prevent sb./sth. from doing sth.	to stop sb. from achieving an aim/sth. from happening	*verhindern, dass jmd. etw. tut/etw. geschieht*
raw material	material before being processed	*Rohstoff*
to reduce sth.	to decrease or make sth. smaller	*verringern, reduzieren*
reduction	the process of making sth. decrease or become smaller	*Reduzierung, Verkleinerung*
reforestation	planting new trees/forests	*Wiederaufforstung*
solar radiation	energy in the form of heat that is sent out from the sun	*Sonneneinstrahlung*
source	the origin of sth.	*Quelle*
to supply the demand for sth.	to produce or deliver enough of sth.	*den Bedarf decken*

unleaded [ˌʌnˈledɪd] **petrol**	unleaded petrol does not contain any lead	*bleifreies Benzin*
water supply	the amount of water that is available to be used	*Wasserversorgung*

English word/phrase	Explanation in English	German equivalent and/or synonym(s)
	pollution	
carbon dioxide [daɪˈɒksaɪd]	the gas produced when animals breathe out, when carbon is burned in the air or when animal or vegetable substances decay	*Kohlendioxid*
to contaminate	to pollute	*verschmutzen*
to corrode sth.	to destroy sth. by chemical action	*korrodieren, zerstören*
depletion [dɪˈpliːʃn] **(of the ozone layer)**	reduction of ...	*Verringerung von ...*
detergent	substance that helps remove dirt	*Reinigungsmittel*
to discharge sth.	to send out	*etwas ablassen*
to dump	to get rid of sth.	*wegwerfen*
dyes [daɪs]	chemicals that are used to dye or colour e.g. textiles	*Färbemittel*
emission	a gas or substance that is sent into the air	*Schadstoffausstoß*
excess packaging	more packaging than necessary/usual/legal	*unnütze/überflüssige Verpackung*
to expose sth./sb. to sth.	to put sb./sth. in a situation where they are not protected from sth. dangerous	*sich etw. (einer Gefahr) aussetzen*

fertilizer	a substance that is added to the soil to make plants grow	*Dünger*
fumes	smoke	*Abgase*
to harm	to hurt/to injure	*verletzen, schaden*
intensive farming	farming practised on small areas of land with high inputs (of fertilizers, etc.)	*intensive Land-wirtschaft*
irrigation	the act of supplying land or crops with water	*künstliche Bewässerung*
landfill	a place where waste is buried under the ground	*Mülldeponie*
to leak oil	to lose oil	*Öl verlieren/lecken*
oil spill	oil that accidentally flows into the ocean, e. g. after an explosion and contaminates the water	*Ölpest*
pesticide ['pestɪsaɪd]	a chemical substance used to kill insects or small animals that destroy crops	*Schädlingsbekämp-fungsmittel*
pollution	the process of making air/water dirty	*Verschmutzung*
residues *(pl.)* ['rezɪdjuːs]	a substance that remains on a surface and cannot be removed easily	*Rückstände*
sewage ['suːɪdʒ] treatment plant	a place where sewage is treated to stop it being harmful	*Kläranlage*
substance	a particular type of solid, liquid or gas	*Substanz*

sulphuric acid [sʌlˌfjʊərɪk ˈæsɪd]	a powerful acid	*Schwefelsäure*
sulphur dioxide	a poisonous gas that is a cause of air pollution in industrial areas	*Schwefeldioxid*
waste	garbage, litter	*Müll*
to waste	to use more of sth. than is necessary	*verschwenden*

English word/phrase	Explanation in English	German equivalent and/or synonym(s)
recycling		
to contribute to sth.	to be one of the causes of sth.	*zu etwas beitragen*
to cope with a problem	to manage or deal with a problem	*mit einem Problem umgehen/ein Problem lösen*
to donate	to give sth., esp. money to a person or an organization in order to help them	*spenden*
ecology	the study of the relationship of plants and living creatures to each other and to their environment	*Ökologie*
ecosystem	a natural unit consisting of all plants, animals and microorganisms in an area functioning together	*Ökosystem*
energy-efficient	without wasting energy	*energieeffizient*

geothermal energy	energy relating to or coming from the heat inside the earth	*Erdwärme*
metal scrap	metal that is no longer used for the purpose it was made for but can be used again in another way	*Metallschrott*
mixed (loads of) litter	waste of different materials, e. g. paper, plastic, metal, etc.	*unsortierter Müll*
paper processing	the reuse of old paper	*Altpapierverwertung*
to recover sth.	to get sth. that was lost	*etw. zurückgewinnen*
to recycle waste	to pass a substance through a system that enables all or part of that substance to be reused	*Müll/Abfall wiederverwerten*
redevelopment	changing an area by building new roads, houses, factories, etc.	*Veränderung; Entwickung*
renewable	renewable energy replaces itself naturally	*erneuerbar*
to reprocess sth.	to recycle sth.	*etwas wiederverwerten*
returnable	able to be taken or given back	*umtauschbar*
to reuse	to use sth. again	*wiederverwerten*
rubble	broken stones or bricks from a destroyed or damaged building	*Geröll*
sewage treatment plant	a place where sewage is treated to stop it being harmful	*Kläranlage*

solar energy	light and heat of the sun that is used to produce energy	*Sonnenenergie*
sort line	a system of making waste move past a line of workers who sort out recyclable materials	*Müllsortierungsanlage (Fließband)*
to sort rubbish	to separate different waste	*Müll trennen*
sustainable	involving the use of natural products that do not harm the environment	*nachhaltig*

English word/phrase	Explanation in English	German equivalent and/or synonym(s)
(eco-)fashion • (ethical) clothing • business ethics		
animal tissue	the skin of animals	*Leder*
apparel [ə'pærel]	clothing when it is sold in shops	*Kleidung*
brand	a type of product from a particular company	*Marke*
business ethics	business that involves certain moral standards (e. g. fair trade, equal pay, etc.)	*ethische Geschäftspraktiken*
casual wear	comfortable clothes that you wear in your free time	*Freizeitkleidung*
to craft sth.	to make sth. using special skills, esp. with your hands	*etw. handwerklich herstellen*
custom-made	designed and made for a particular person/customer	*maßgefertigt, maßgeschneidert*

to dye sth. [daɪ]	to give sth. a different colour	*etwas färben*
fabric	material made by weaving wool, cotton, silk, etc.	*Gewebe*
fashion victim	a person who always wears the newest fashions even if they do not suit him/her	*jmd., der immer nach dem neuesten Modetrend gekleidet sein möchte*
garment	an item of clothing	*Kleidungsstück*
to grow cotton	to plant and raise cotton	*Baumwolle anbauen*
high(er) end product	sth. that is expensive and of high quality	*ein hochwertiges Markenprodukt*
locally produced	produced in the country/town where the fashion is designed, not outsourced to e.g. China	*aus heimischer Herstellung*
mass production	the production of goods in large quantities	*Massenherstellung*
natural fibres	cloth that is made from natural material, e.g. cotton, silk	*natürliche Materialien*
ready-made	made in standard sizes, not to the measurements of a particular customer	*Massenware, Konfektionsware*
to sew [səʊ]	to use a needle and thread to make stitches in cloth	*nähen*
social responsibility	taking care of people and their physical and economic well-being	*soziale Verantwortung*

sweatshop	place where people work for low wages in poor conditions	*eine Fabrik, die schlechte Arbeitsbedingungen hat und unfaire (extrem niedrige) Löhne zahlt*
synthetic fibre	a garment made of synthetic fibres is made of artificial substances (and not cotton, wool, etc.)	*Kunstfaser, Chemiefaser*
textile finishing	process to give the surface of a textile a special appearance and higher quality	*Textilveredlung*
textile processing	the (industrial) production of textiles	*Textilverarbeitung*
vintage	classic, showing the best characteristics of its kind	here: *aus einer bestimmten Zeit, klassisch*
work ethics	working conditions that involve moral principles (e.g. no exploitation, fair wages, etc.)	*ethische Arbeitsbedingungen*

English word/phrase	Explanation in English	German equivalent and/or synonym(s)
consumerism • consumption		
availability	the fact that someone is free to work, be contacted, etc. or whether or how much they can	*Verfügbarkeit*
to be available to sb.	able to be reached by sb.	*erhältlich, verfügbar für jmd. sein*

consumer	sb. who buys and uses products and services	*Konsument*
customer	sb. who buys goods or services from a shop, company etc.	*Kunde*
developing country	a country which is poor and tries to make its industry and economic system more advanced	*Entwicklungsland*
discount shopping	to go shopping at a store that sells goods cheaply	*im Discounter einkaufen*
to display sth.	to present sth.	*etw. anzeigen*
distribution of sth.	the act of sharing things among a large group of people	*Verteilung*
efficiency	the quality of doing sth. well without wasting money or time	*Effizienz, Leistungsfähigkeit*
fair trade	involving trade which supports producers in developing countries by paying fair prices and making sure that workers have good working conditions and fair payment	*fairer Handel*
industrialized mass production	when products are made in large numbers by industrial machines so they can be sold cheaply	*industrialisierte Massenproduktion*
Internet retailer	Internet shop	*Internethändler*

mounting consumer debt	strongly rising consumer debt	*steigende Konsumverschuldung*
online shopping portal	a website where you can buy things by choosing them online	*online Einkaufsportal*
price spiral [spaɪrəl]	a rise in prices	*Preisspirale*
purchasing power	the amount of money a person or group has available to spend	*Kaufkraft*
shipping	the delivery of goods	*Lieferung, Verschiffung*
status symbol	sth. that you have or own that shows high social rank or position	*Statussymbol*
range of products	selection of products	*Produktumfang*

English word/phrase	Explanation in English	German equivalent and/or synonym(s)
	ecology • energy	
agriculture	the practice of farming	*Landwirtschaft*
biodegradable [ˌbaɪəʊdɪˈgreɪdəbl]	changed naturally by bacteria into substances that do not harm the environment	*biologisch abbaubar*
carbon emission	carbon dioxide that planes, cars, factories, etc. produce, which is harmful to the environment	*Kohlenstoffausstoß*
climate change	a permanent change in weather conditions	*Klimawandel*
crops	plants that are grown by farmers and used as food	*Ernten*

deforestation	the cutting or burning down of all the trees in an area	*Waldrodung*
to dump sth.	to throw sth. away	*etw. wegschmeißen*
exploitation	an unfair treatment – used to show disapproval	*Ausbeutung*
fragility of sth.	easily broken or damaged	*Zerbrechlichkeit*
fossil [ˈfɒsl] **fuel**	fuel such as coal and oil, which was formed underground from plant and animal remains millions of years ago	*fossiler Brennstoff*
global warming	the increase in temperature of the earth's atmosphere, caused by the increase of particular gases, esp. CO_2	*globale Erwärmung*
habitat	natural home of a plant or animal	*Lebensraum*
to have an impact on sth.	to influence sth.	*etw. beeinflussen*
the incineration of trash	the act of burning trash in a facility	*Müllverbrennung*
nuclear energy	powerful form of energy produced by splitting nuclei of atoms	*Atomenergie; nukleare Energie*
to pose a threat for/to sb.	to be regarded as a possible danger for/to sb.	*für jdn. eine Bedrohung darstellen*

renewable energies	types of energy such as wind or solar power that can be replaced naturally	*erneuerbare Energien*
sustainability	ability to continue for a long time without causing damage to the environment	*Nachhaltigkeit*
techniques [tekˈniːk] **of cultivation**	techniques of using land	*Anbautechniken*
waste disposal	garbage disposal	*Müllentsorgung*
water supply	the water that is provided and treated for a particular area	*Wasserversorgung*

The Global Challenge – Economy Worldwide

English word/phrase	Explanation in English	German equivalent and/or synonym(s)
	globalisation	
capital market	financial market	*Finanzmarkt, Kapitalmarkt*
cultural imperialism	the imposing of a foreign culture on sb.	*kultureller Imperialismus*
domestic demand	the amount of money that is spent on goods and services by the people, companies, and government within a particular country	*inländische Nachfrage*
domestic labour	the working situation within a particular country	*inländischer Arbeitsmarkt*
economic tie	economic connection to sb.	*Wirtschaftsverbindung*
entrepreneurship [ˌɒntrəprəˈnɜː(r)ʃɪp]	running one's own business	*Unternehmertum*
expatriate	a person living (and working) in a country that is not their own	*jmd., der sein Heimatland verlässt, um Arbeit zu finden*
to generate capital	to earn money	*Kapital erzeugen (Geld verdienen)*
global labour market	global workforce	*globaler Arbeitsmarkt*
infrastructure	the basic systems and services, such as transport or power supplies that a country or organization uses in order to work effectively	*Infrastruktur*

interdependency	a situation in which people or things depend on each other	*Korrelation, gegenseitige Abhängigkeit*
international trade	trade between different countries	*internationaler Handel*
to be internationalized	to make sth. become international	*internationalisiert sein*
to invest in sb./sth./ investment in	to spend money on sth. in order to gain sth. back	*in etw./jmd. investieren; Investition in*
labour standards	the working conditions	*Arbeitsgesetzgebung*
liberalization of sth.	the act of making sth. less strict	*Liberalisierung von etw.*
logistics	the practical organization of sth.	*Logistik*
microcredit [ˈmɒɪkrəʊˌkredɪt]	a small credit	*Mikrokredit, Kleinkredit*
microloan [ˈmɒɪkrəʊləʊn]	a very small credit given to sb.	*Mikrokredit, Kleinkredit*
multinationals	internationally cooperating companies	*multinationale Konzerne*
output	the amount of sth. that a company produces	*Produktion, Leistung*
to outsource	to arrange for sb. outside a company to do work or provide goods for that company	*auslagern*
to promote international trade	to do sth. in order to increase the international trade	*internationalen Handel fördern*

protectionism	when a government tries to help industries in its own country by taxing or restricting goods	*Protektionismus, Schutzpolitik*
to raise living-standards	to level up the comfort and the amount of money that people have	*Lebensstandards erhöhen*
repatriate	a person who has lived and worked abroad and now returns to his homeland	*Rückkehrer in sein Heimatland*
standardized	all the things of one particular type made the same as each other	*standardisiert*
sweatshop ['swet ʃɑp]	a small factory where workers are paid very little and work many hours in very bad conditions	*Ausbeuterbetrieb*
trade negotiation	discussion about economic affairs in order to reach an agreement	*Wirtschafts-verhandlung(en)*
uniformity	the quality of being or looking the same as all members of a group	*Einheitlichkeit;* standardization

English word/phrase	Explanation in English	German equivalent and/or synonym(s)
politics • constitution • political systems		
administration	government, organization	*Regierung, Verwaltung*

(to come to an) agreement	a decision or arrangement, often formal and written, between two or more groups of people	*sich einigen*
amendment	a change to a law that is still being discussed	*Zusatz (zur Verfassung)*
to carry a decision	to accept a decision	*einen Entscheid annehmen/mittragen*
to confirm sth.	to say that sth. is definitely true	*bestätigen*
consent [kən'sent]	agreement	*Einvernehmen, Einverständnis*
Constitution	a set of basic laws and principles that a country or organization is governed by	*Verfassung*
domestic policy	the internal policy of a country without involving other countries	*Innenpolitik*
foreign policy	involving or dealing with other countries	*Außenpolitik*
Foreign Secretary	the British politician who is in charge of the Foreign Office and the political relationship with other countries	*Außenminister(in)*
to set up a government	to organize/arrange a government	*eine Regierung aufstellen*
to govern	to rule	*regieren*
Head of State	the main representative of a country, such as a king, queen etc	*Staatsoberhaupt*

to interfere with sth.	to prevent sth. from happening the way that it was planned	*sich einmischen*
policy	a set of ideas of what to do in particular situations that has been agreed officially by a government or a political party	*eine bestimmte Politik*
politician [ˌpɒləˈtɪʃn]	someone who works in politics, especially an elected member of the government	*Politiker*
political [pəˈlɪtɪkl]	relating to governmental actions or people	*politisch*
politics	the activities of the government, members of law-making organizations or people who try to influence the way a country is governed	*Politik im Allgemeinen*
to be politically impartial	not to be in favour of any particular political party	*unparteiisch sein*
(to ratify a) treaty	to make an agreement officially valid	*(einen) Vertrag (unterzeichnen)*
universal suffrage	the right of all the people in the country to vote	*allgemeines Wahlrecht*

English word/phrase	Explanation in English	German equivalent and/or synonym(s)
crises • war • poverty		
to accomplish a mission	to succeed in doing sth.	*eine Mission erfüllen*

combat	fighting, esp. during a war	*Kampf; Gefecht*
civil war	a war in which opposing groups of people from the same country fight each other in order to gain political control	*Bürgerkrieg*
crisis (crises) ['kraɪsɪs]	situation(s) in which there are a lot of problems that must be dealt with quickly so that it cannot get any worse	*Krise (Krisen)*
to declare war on sb.	to start a war against someone	*jdm. den Krieg erklären*
to fall into poverty	to become poor	*in Armut abstürzen*
to invade	to enter a country using military force in order to control it	*eindringen, überfallen*
invasion of a country	when the army of one country enters another country by force, in order to take control of it	*Überfall, Einmarsch in ein Land*
to occupy ['ɒkjupaɪ]	to enter a place in a large group and keep control of it	*belagern, besetzen*
occupant	member of the occupying force	*Besatzer*
occupation of ['ɒkju'peɪʃn]	when a large group of people enter a place and take control of it, especially by military force	*Besatzung*
to withdraw/ withdrawal	to stop taking part in an activity	*sich zurückziehen; Rückzug*

English word/phrase	Explanation in English	German equivalent and/or synonym(s)
the United Nations		
to adopt (a charter)	to formally approve sth., especially by voting	*eine Charta verabschieden*
annual session	a session which happens every year	*jährliche Sitzung*
collective military action	a military action that is done or shared by every member of a group	*gemeinsame militärische Aktion*
diplomacy [dɪˈpləʊməsi]	the job or activity of managing the relationships between countries	*Diplomatie*
to enforce sth.	to make sth. happen or force sb. to do sth.	*etw. durchsetzen;* to put sth. into effect
General Assembly	the group that represents all of the countries which belong to the United Nations	*Vollversammlung*
to impose sanctions	to start using official orders or laws as a way of forcing e. g. a leader of another country to make political changes	*Sanktionen verhängen*
to lay out an agenda	to present an agenda clearly and carefully	*ein Programm aufstellen/darlegen*
to maintain peace	to make peace continue	*Frieden aufrechterhalten/erhalten*

to mediate between	to try to end a disagreement between two or more people or groups by talking to them	*vermitteln*
to provide sth.	to give sth. to sb. or make it available for them to use	*etwas bereitstellen*
trade embargo	trade boycott	*Handelsembargo, Handelssperre*
tribunal [traɪˈbjuːnl]	a type of court that is given official authority to deal with a problem	*Tribunal, Gericht*

English word/phrase	Explanation in English	German equivalent and/or synonym(s)
urbanization		
to accommodate/ accommodation	to provide sb. with a room or place to sleep or live	*jdn. unterbringen/ beherbergen; Unterbringung*
communal	shared by or for the use of a number of people, esp. people who live together	*gemeinsam*
decentralization [ˌdiːˌsentrəlaɪˈzeɪʃn]	the act of moving parts of a government, organization, etc. from a central place to several different smaller ones	*Dezentralisierung*
degradation	the process of sth. being damaged or made worse	*Degradierung, Abbau*
façade [fəˈsɑːd]	the front of a building	*Fassade*

gated community	a group of houses surrounded by a wall or fence, with an entrance that is guarded	*bewachtes Wohnviertel*
(historical/cultural) heritage	the traditional beliefs, values, customs, etc. of a family, country, or society	*(historisches/ kulturelles) Erbe*
intergenerational	between or involving people from different age groups	*generations-übergreifend*
metropolitan	connected with a large or capital city	*hauptstädtisch/ großstädtisch*
municipal	connected to a city, town	*städtisch, Stadt-, kommunal*
occupation *(fml.)*	the act of living in a building/area, etc.	*Besitz, Bewohnen*
to occupy	to live or stay in a place	*bewohnen; to inhabit*
pedestrian zone	a shopping area in the centre of a town where cars, trucks, etc. cannot go	*Fußgängerzone*
public transport	buses, trains, etc. that are available for everyone to use	*öffentliche Verkehrs-mittel*
resident	sb. who lives in a particular place or who has their home there	*Bewohner*
residential area	a residential area consists of private houses rather than offices or factories	*Wohngegend*
skyscraper	a very tall modern city building	*Wolkenkratzer*
(social) equity	fairness	*(soziale) Gerechtigkeit*

suburban	in or connected with an area where people live that is outside the centre of a city	*Vorstadt-*
urban/urbanization	relating to towns and cities/the process by which more and more people live and work in towns and cities rather than in the countryside	*städtisch/Verstädte-rung*

English word/phrase	Explanation in English	German equivalent and/or synonym(s)
megacities		
corrugated iron shacks	very small and simple buildings made from pieces of corrugated metal or other materials	*Wellblechhütten*
densely populated	containing a lot of people living with little space between them	*dicht bevölkert*
deterioration [dɪˈtɪərɪəˈreɪʃn]	the act of becoming worse	*Verfall, Verschlech-terung*
economic concentra-tion	a large amount of economy in a particular place	*Wirtschaftskonzen-tration*
expansion of city boundaries	the process by which a city increases in size	*Ausweitung von Stadtgrenzen*
housing	the houses, flats, apartments, etc. that people live in	*Unterkunft, Unter-bringung*
increase	growth	*Wachstum*

inefficient [ˌɪnɪˈfɪʃnt]	not doing a job well and making poor use of time, energy, etc.	*ineffizient, unwirtschaftlich*
(massive) infrastructure	the basic system and services that are necessary for a country or an organization to run smoothly	*(starke) Infrastruktur*
megacity	a city of over 10 million inhabitants	*Millionenstadt, Metropole*
population density	the degree to which an area is filled with people	*Bevölkerungsdichte*
slum dweller	sb. who lives in a slum	*Slumbewohner*
social unrest	a political situation in which people are angry and likely to protest or fight	*soziale Unruhe(n)*

English word/phrase	Explanation in English	German equivalent and/or synonym(s)
society • values		
accessible [əkˈsesəbl]	able to be reached	*verfügbar, zugänglich*
civic duties	sth. you have to do because it is morally or legally right	*staatsbürgerliche Pflichten*
discriminatory [dɪˈskrɪmɪnətəri]	treating sb. or a group of people worse than others in an unfair way	*diskriminierend*
discrimination of sb.	the practice of treating sb. or a particular group in society less fairly than others	*Diskriminierung von jmdm.*

diversity [daɪˈvɜːsəti]	a range of different people, things or ideas	*Vielfalt*
freedom of expression	the freedom to say or write what you think or feel	*Freiheit der Meinungs-äußerung*
fundamentalism [ˌfʌndəˈmentəlɪzəm]	the practice of following very strictly the basic rules of any religion	*Fundamentalismus*
internal (social) stability	the maintenance, constancy and reliability of social systems, e. g. patterns of relationships like family, work, business, etc.	*innere (soziale) Stabilität*
limitation	restriction	*Begrenzung, Einschränkung*
prejudice [ˈpredʒʊdɪs]	an unreasonable dislike and distrust of people who are different from you in some way	*Vorurteil*
to be prejudiced	having an unreason-able dislike of or preference for sb./sth.	*voreingenommen sein*
religious community	a group of people who have the same religion	*religiöse Gemeinschaft*

All the World's a Stage: Art and Literature

English word/phrase	Explanation in English	German equivalent and/or synonym(s)
	Shakespeare's theatre	
blank verse	poetry that has a regular rhythm, usually ten syllables and five stresses, but which does not rhyme	*Blankvers (reimloser, fünfhebiger, jambischer Vers)*
censorship	the practice or system of censoring and controlling sth.	*Zensur*
to deal with a theme	to be about a theme	*ein Thema behandeln, von einem Thema handeln*
dramatist	someone who writes plays, especially serious ones	*Dramatiker*
figurative ['fɪgərətɪv]	symbolic	*symbolisch*
first edition	first printed version of a play	*Erstausgabe*
gallery	upstairs areas in the theatre	*Balkon, Empore*
groundlings	poorest theatregoers who stood in the open yard in front of the stage	*unter freiem Himmel stehende Zuschauer, Stehplätze*
history play	historical drama	*historisches Schauspiel*
metaphorical	connected with or containing metaphors	*methaphorisch*
play on words, pun	an amusing use of a word or phrase that has two meanings	*Wortspiel*

prose	writing that is not poetry	*Prosa (ungebundene Rede)*
playwright	writer of plays	*Dramatiker*
to produce a play	to make a play	*ein Schauspiel produzieren*
repertory ['repətri]	collection of plays, pieces of music, etc. that a performer or theatre company has learnt and can perform	*Repertoire, Repertoiretheater*
theatre company	group of people (actors, playwright, etc.) that work together at a theatre	*Theaterensemble, Schauspieltruppe*
the wooden O	nickname given to the Globe Theatre because of its circular shape	*„das hölzerne O" (Spitzname des Globe Theaters aufgrund seiner runden Form)*

English word/phrase	Explanation in English	German equivalent and/or synonym(s)
	Elizabethan England	
age of (scientific) invention	a particular period in history	*neues (wissenschaftliches) Zeitalter, Zeitalter der Erfindungen*
corporal punishment	physical punishment	*körperliche Bestrafung (Auspeitschen, an den Pranger stellen, brandmarken etc.)*
era of trans-Atlantic trade	establishment of overseas trading posts (e.g. West Indies, North America, etc.)	*Ära des transatlantischen Handels*

Protestantism	the only legal form of religion permitted in Elizabethan England	*Protestantismus*
public execution	the act of killing sb in public, especially as a legal punishment	*öffentliche Hinrichtung*
Reformation	new ideas in religion in 16th-cen-tury Europe that led to attempts to reform the Roman Catholic Church and to the formation of the Protestant Churches	*Reformation (wörtl. Erneuerung)*
Renaissance [rɪ'neɪsns]	the period in Europe during the 14th, 15th and 16th centuries when people became interested in the ancient cultures of Greece and Rome	*Renaissance (Neuzeit)*
(defeat of) Spanish Armada	(1588) high point of Elizabeth's reign; most powerful European sea power	*(der Sieg über die) spanische Armada*
superstition	belief in supernatural forces	*Aberglaube*
the "golden age"	flowering of poetry, music, and literature	*goldenes Zeitalter*
Tudor ['tjuːdə(r)]	connected with the time when the kings and queens of the Tudor family ruled England (1485 – 1603)	*Tudor (royaler Familienname)*

English word/phrase	Explanation in English	German equivalent and/or synonym(s)
	arts	
abstract painting	a painting that does not picture things or people in a realistic way	*abstraktes Gemälde*
the arts	art, music, theatre, film, literature etc. all considered together	*die Künste*
art dealer	a person that trades in art	*Kunsthändler*
artist	sb. who produces art	*Künstler*
art movements	groups of artists which have similar ideas and interests in style	*Künstlerbewegungen*
bright/radiant colours	intensive/glowing colours	*leuchtende Farben*
brush stroke	the way in which paint is put onto a surface with a brush	*Pinselstrich*
canvas	a painting done with oil paints, or the piece of cloth it is painted on	*Leinwand*
charcoal drawing	a picture drawn with a hard black substance similar to coal	*Kohlezeichnung*
colour scheme	a combination of colours that has been chosen for a painting	*Farbabstimmung*
contemporary	existing or happening now	*zeitgenössisch*

covering application (of paint)	the act of painting e. g. a wall in a way that underlying paint or structures aren't visible anymore	*deckender Farbauftrag*
dab of colour	quick light touches of colour	*Farbtupfer*
drawing	a picture made with a pen or pencil	*Zeichnung*
etching	a picture made by printing from an etched metal plate	*Radierung*
figurative painting/ portrayal	the act of showing or describing objects or people, etc. in a picture, play, book, etc.	*figürliche Darstellung*
foreground	the people, objects, etc. in a picture that seem nearest to you and form its main part	*Vordergrund*
masterpiece	a work of art that is of very high quality	*Meisterwerk*
mixture/composition of colours	the act of mixing and using colours	*Farbmischung, Farbkomposition*
modernism	art movement	*Moderne*
oil on canvas	oil painting	*Öl auf Leinwand*
oil painting	a painting done with oil paints	*Ölgemälde*
painter	someone who paints pictures	*Maler*
pastel ['pæstl] **drawing**	a picture drawn with colours that are light and pale	*Pastellzeichnung*

to perform sth.	to do sth. to entertain people	*etw. vorführen/ aufführen*
performance	the act of performing a play or a piece of music, also the way sb. performs	*Performanz, Aufführung*
performing arts	arts such as dance, music or drama	*darstellende Künste*
picture size/format	the size of a painting	*Bildformat, Bildgröße*
piece of art	sth. that has been produced by an artist	*Kunstwerk*
print	letters, numbers, words or symbols that have been produced on paper by a machine using ink (= Tinte)	*Druck*
reflection of light	the action or process of light being thrown back from a surface	*Lichtreflektion*
reproduction	copy of a work of art	*Reproduktion, Vervielfältigung*
sculptor	sb. who makes sculptures out of stone, wood etc	*Bildhauer*
shade	the dark places in a picture or painting	*Schattierung*
spatial perspective	perspective relating to the position, size, shape etc. of things	*räumliche Perspektive*
to have a talent for sth.	to be naturally good at sth.	*ein Talent für etwas haben*
transparent/ translucent	if sth. is transparent, you can see through it very clearly	*durchscheinend*

two-dimensional (portrayal)	flat portrayal without depth, does not seem real	*flächige Darstellung*
work of art	if a painting, design etc works, it is successful because it has the effect on you that the artist intended	*Kunstwerk*

The Culture Industry: Perception, Persuasion & Promises in the Media

English word/phrase	Explanation in English	German equivalent and/or synonym(s)
mass media		
commercialization [kəˌmɜːʃəlaɪˈzeɪʃn]	the process of making profit from sth. and being more interested in profit than in the values/quality of sth.	*Kommerzialisierung*
to cover a subject	to report on an event for TV, a newspaper, etc.	*über etw. berichten*
documentary	a film giving facts about sth.	*Dokumentarfilm*
edutainment	products such as books, TV programs and esp. computer software that both educate and entertain	*Unterhaltungspro-gramm, Computerspiel etc. mit Lernfaktor*
factual report	a report based on or containing facts	*Tatsachenbericht*
to have access to sth.	to have the opportu-nity or right to use or to see sth.	*zu etwas Zugang haben*
infotainment	TV programs etc. that present news and serious subjects in an entertaining way	*unterhaltsame Informationssendung z. B. für Kinder*
to invade sb.'s privacy	to affect sb.'s privacy in an unpleasant or annoying way	*in jds. Privatssphäre eindringen*

live coverage	a report on television or radio that is seen or heard at the same time as it is actually happening	*Direktübertragung*
on the net	on the Internet	*im Internet*
to post sth. online	to put sth. on a website	*im Internet veröffent-lichen*
to release sth.	to publish sth.	*etw. veröffentlichen, herausgeben*
safeguard	sth. that is designed to protect sth. from harm, danger, etc.	*Sicherheitsvorkehrung*
sitcom *(abbr.)*	situational comedy	*Sitcom, Fernseh-komödie*
social networking/ social networks	a system of trying to meet and talk to other people through the Internet	*soziale Netzwerke*
soap (opera)	a story about the lives and problems of a group of people, which is broadcast every day on television or radio	*Seifenoper*
to surf the Internet	to visit a lot of websites	*im Internet surfen*
surveillance [sɜːˈveɪləns]	the act of carefully watching a person suspected of a crime	*Überwachung; observation*
source of information	the place where sb. finds information	*Informationsquelle*
virus [ˈvaɪrəs]	instructions that are hidden in a computer program and are designed to cause faults or destroy data	*Computervirus*

English word/phrase	Explanation in English	German equivalent and/or synonym(s)
the press		
attention-grabbing	attracting the attention of sb. in a rather spectacular way, e. g. by very large or provocative headlines or photographs	*anreißerisch, aufsehenheischend*
balanced	keeping or showing a balance so that different things or different parts of sth. exist in equal or correct amounts	*ausgewogen, neutral*
breaking news	news that has just occurred	*Eilmeldung, Sondermeldung*
broadcasting company	a company whose business is to make and send out radio and television programmes	*Fernseh-/Radiosender*
censorship	the act or policy of removing parts from a book, film/movie etc. which are considered to be offensive, immoral or a political threat	*Zensur*
coverage	the reporting of news in newspapers, radio or TV	*Berichterstattung*
to cover a subject	to report on sth.	*von etw. berichten*
code of ethics	a set of moral principles or rules of behaviour	*ethischer Kodex*

current affairs	events of political or social importance that are happening now	*Tagesgeschehen*
editorial	an important article in a newspaper, that expresses the editor's opinion about an item of news or an issue	*Leitartikel*
factual (information)	based on or containing facts	*Sachinformation*
freedom of the press	the legal right to write or say what you want	*Pressefreiheit*
gossip	informal talk or stories about other people's private lifes, often including unkind or untrue remarks	*Klatsch (-presse)*
hard news	facts, factual information	*Fakten*
letter to the editor	a letter sent to a publication, e.g. a magazine or (online) newspaper, about issues of concern from its readers	*Leserbrief an den Herausgeber*
private sector broadcaster	private broadcasting companies	*private Fernsehanstalt*
public sector broadcaster	public broadcasting companies	*öffentlich-rechtliche Fernsehanstalt*
to publish	to produce a book, magazine, CD-ROM, etc. and sell it to the public; to print a letter, an article, etc. in a newspaper or a magazine	*veröffentlichen*

popular newspaper/ tabloid	a newspaper with small pages, short simple reports and a lot of pictures and stories about famous people, often thought of as less serious than other newspapers	*Boulevardzeitung*
quality newspaper/ broadsheet	a newspaper printed in a large size, generally considered more serious than smaller newspapers	*seriöse Zeitung*
sensationalist [sen'seɪʃənəlɪst]	provoking public interest or excitement by reporting facts in a way that makes them seem as strange or shocking as possible	*sensationslüstern, effekthascherisch*

English word/phrase	Explanation in English	German equivalent and/or synonym(s)
communication		
to communicate with sb.	to exchange information, news, ideas, etc. with sb.	*kommunizieren*
communications systems	systems, that are used to send information, especially telephones, radio, computers, etc.	*Kommunikationsmittel*
data ['deɪtə, 'dɑːtə]	facts or information, especially when examined and used to find out things or to make decisions	*Daten*
data theft	the act of stealing data	*Datendiebstahl*

to distribute sth. (via the Internet)	to send information using a particular way/method	*etw. (über das Internet) verbreiten*
to process sth.	to deal officially with a document, request, etc. in the usual way; to deal with information using a computer	*etw. verarbeiten*
to transfer data	to move information from one place to another	*Daten übertragen*
wireless communication	a system of sending and receiving signals that does not use wires	*drahtlose Kommunikation*
word processing	the use of a computer to create, store and print a piece of text	*Textverarbeitung*

English word/phrase	Explanation in English	German equivalent and/or synonym(s)
	arts	
the arts	art, music, theatre, film, literature etc all considered together	*die Künste*
art dealer	a person that buys and sells art	*Kunsthändler*
art movements	groups of artists which have similar ideas and interests in style	*Künstlerbewegungen*
bright/radiant colours	intensive/glowing colours	*leuchtende Farben*
contemporary	existing or happening now	*zeitgenössisch*

drawing	a picture made with a pen or pencil	*Zeichnung*
etching	a picture made by printing from an etched metal plate	*Radierung*
figurative painting	a type of art that shows objects, people, or the countryside as they really look	*figurative Malerei*
masterpiece	a work of art that is of very high quality	*Meisterwerk*
modernism	art movement	*Moderne*
piece of art	sth. that has been produced by an artist	*Kunstwerk*
photographer [fəˈtɒgrəfə(r)]	someone who takes photographs	*Fotograf*
portrait [ˈpɔːtreɪt]	a painting, drawing, or photograph of a person	*Porträt*
reflexion of light	the action or process of light being thrown back from a surface	*Lichtreflektion*
sculptor	someone who makes sculptures out of stone, wood etc.	*Bildhauer*
visual arts	art such as painting and sculpture etc. that you look at, as opposed to literature or music	*bildende Künste*

work of art	if a painting, design etc. works, it is successful because it has the effect on you that the artist intended	*Kunstwerk*

English word/phrase	Explanation in English	German equivalent and/or synonym(s)
culture		
auction/to auction sth.	a public meeting where things are sold to the person who offers the most money for them	*Versteigerung; versteigern*
box-office hit	a successful film measured by the number of people who pay to see it	*Kassenschlager*
collection/collector	a set of similar things that are kept or brought together because they are attractive or interesting	*Sammlung; Sammler*
demand for sth.	the need or desire that people have for particular goods and services	*Nachfrage nach*
mass culture	intended for a large number of people	*Massenkultur*
promoter/to promote sb./sth.	sb. who tries to encourage something to happen or develop	*Veranstalter/in, Förderer; jdn./etw. fördern*

Advertising Terms

to address sb.	to say sth. directly to sb.
advertisement/ad	a paid message in which the sponsor is identified; *Werbung/ Werbeanzeige*
to put an advertisement in a paper	*eine Werbeanzeige veröffentlichen (in einer Zeitung)*
advertising agency/campaign/ space/expert	*Werbeagentur/-kampagne/-platz/ -experte*
A I D A *(abbr.)*	(gain) **A**ttention (hold) **I**nterest (arouse) **D**esire (encourage to take) **A**ction
to appeal to sb./appealing	to be interesting, attractive (to sb.)
art director [daɪˈrektə(r), dɪ-]	an ad agency employee for designing and producing the artwork and layout
article on/about sth.	a piece of writing often in a magazine/newspaper
artificial/artificiality [ˌɑːˈtɪˈfɪʃl/ˌɑːtɪˌfɪʃiˈæləti]	made or produced to copy sth. natural; not real; *künstlich*
at first sight; at first glance	*auf den ersten Blick*
to attract sb.'s attention	*jdns. Interesse wecken*
audiovisual presentation	a presentation involving both pictures and spoken words
banner headline	a line of words printed in large letters
B & W	black and white ad
bold; heavy-faced type	in a thick, dark type; *fettgedruckt, in Fettdruck*
billboard/billboard advertising	*große Reklamefläche*
body copy	the main part of the reading matter of an ad

brand	a label by which a product is identified; *Marke(nname)*
brand image (personality)	the pattern of feelings, ideas and images held by the public with regard to a specific brand
brand loyalty	the tendency of customers to continue buying the same brand
brochure ['brəʊʃə(r)]	a booklet promoting products or services
capital letter	*Großbuchstabe*
caption ['kæpʃn]	text written underneath a picture to explain it
client ['klaɪənt]	customer; *Kunde*
clumsy	not well designed
column ['kɒləm]	*Textspalte*
competition/competitor [ˌkɒmpə'tɪʃn/kəm'petɪtə(r)]	*Wettbewerb/Wettbewerber*
consumer advertising	advertising of products sold to the general public
to convince sb./conviction [ˌkən'vɪns/kən'vɪkʃn]	to make sb. believe that sth. is true by giving arguments; *jdn. überzeugen/Überzeugung*
to carry conviction	to be/sound convincing
copy	any word or text material for publication, broadcast or production
copywriter	a person who writes advertising; *Werbetexter*
to be creative; to work creatively	*kreativ sein; kreativ arbeiten*
creative director	ad agency employee responsible for supervising the work of copywriters, etc.

direct response	specified advertising to reach individual customers (e. g. enquiry card system)
editor	a person who is in charge of a newspaper, etc; *Herausgeber; Redakteur*
to evoke (interest in sth.)	*(Interesse an) etwas wecken/ hervorrufen*
exaggerated [ɪgˈzædʒəreɪtɪd]	*übertrieben*
eye-catcher	*Blickfang*
eye appeal	*Werbewirksamkeit*
electronic media	*elektronische Medien*
digital media	*digitale Medien*
field of vision	*Blickfeld*
flashy	attracting attention by being bright, large, etc.
folder/folding	a folded brochure/sth. that can be folded, e. g. a brochure
front page	first page of a newspaper/ magazine
four colour	artwork reproduced in full colour
to glance at	to look quickly at sth.
to glamorize	to make sth. appear attractive, beautiful, romantic
grouped style	*Blocksatz*
hitting (making) the headlines	*Schlagzeilen machen*
illustration (picture)	Illustration
image	the public's perception of a company or product
industrial advertising	advertising of industrial products
jingle [ˈdʒɪŋgl]	music and lyrics used in a commercial

label	*Etikett, Beschriftung*
layout	arrangement of sth.
logo	the name and/or symbol of a company set in a specially designed lettering
market	population representing potential customers
marketing/marketing communications	an event or occasion, usually held at regular intervals, at which people meet for the purpose of buying and selling merchandise
media	*die Medien*
merchandising	activities designed to promote retail sales
objective	what you want to accomplish; *Ziel*
passage, paragraph	*Abschnitt*
to persuade sb./persuasion [pə'sweɪd/pə'sweɪʒn]	*jdn. überreden/Überredung*
persuasive(ly)	being able to make sb. do or believe sth.
point of purchase	displays in stores designed to catch the customers' attention
portfolio	presentation folder containing samples *(Muster)*
premium	a gift offered to potential customers
prime time	peak viewing time, time when the greatest numbers of people are watching TV/listening to the radio
print media	*Druckmedien (Zeitschriften, Magazine etc.)*
press	*Presse*
press release/news release	written news information mailed to the media

promotion	activities used to encourage the purchase of a product
psychographics ['saɪkəʊ'græfɪks]	statistics relating to the personalities, attitudes and life-styles of people and used as a tool in marketing
public relations (PR)	activity of influencing the press so that they print stories that promote a company/a product
reply card	a self-addressed postcard
(to do) research	careful study of a subject in order to discover new facts/information
to skim a text	to read sth. quickly/superficially
to scan a text	to read quickly but not very carefully
to seduce/seduction [sɪ'djuːs/sɪ'dʌkʃn]	*verführen/Verführung*
slogan	a word or phrase that is easy to remember esp. in advertising
strategy	a plan to achieve a particular purpose
subconscious(ly)	*unterbewusst*
subheadline/-heading	title given to a part of an article
supplement ['sʌplɪmənt]	an extra separate section that is sold with the newspaper/magazine; *Beilage*
sweepstakes	a sales promotion in which prizes are awarded to the customer; *Preisausschreiben*
tactics	strategy
target group	a particular group of people the advertisement is aimed at; *Zielgruppe*

trade advertising	advertising aimed at wholesalers, distributors and retailers rather than customers
trademark	a name, symbol or design a company uses for its products and that cannot be used by anyone else; *Handelsname, Warenzeichen*
two colour	ad printed in two colours, usually black and a second colour for effect
unconscious(ly) [ʌnˈkɒnʃəs(li)]	without being aware; *unbewusst*

Business, Administration & Finance

accountancy [ə'kaʊnt(ə)nsi]	*Buchführung, Buchhaltung*
accountant [ə'kaʊnt(ə)nt]	*Buchhalter*
acquisition [ˌakwɪ'zɪʃ(ə)n]	*Akquisition, Ankauf*
administration	*Verwaltung*
administrative [əd'mɪnɪstrətɪv]	*verwaltungs-, verwaltungstechnisch*
allocation	*Etat*
assessment	*Bewertung, Begutachtung, Festsetzung*
asset ['asɛt]	*Gewinn, Kapital, Wirtschaftsgut*
boost/to boost	*Aufschwung/fördern*
broker	*Börsenmakler, Handelsmakler*
commodity [kə'mɒdɪti]	*Ware, Handelsware, Produkt*
compensation	*Entschädigung*
competitor/competition [kəm'pɛtɪtə , kəmpɪ'tɪʃ(ə)n]	*Wettbewerber/Wettbewerb*
consultant	*Finanzberater, Gutachter*
consumer/to consume [kən'sjuːmə, kən'sjuːm]	*Konsument/konsumieren*
consumption [kən'sʌm(p)ʃ(ə)n]	*Konsum*
contract/contractor	*Vertrag/Vertragsschließender/ Auftragnehmer/Subunternehmer*
corporation	*Gesellschaft, Unternehmen*
creditor	*Gläubiger, Kreditgeber*
debtor	*Darlehensnehmer, Kreditnehmer, Schuldner*
deficit	*Fehlbetrag, Minusbetrag, Rückstand*
depreciation [dɪˌpriːʃɪ'eɪʃ(ə)n]	*Abschreibung, Minderung des Wertes*

directive [dɪˈrɛktɪv]	*Betriebsanweisung, Verfügung, Vereinbarung*
to dismiss/dismissal	*jdn. entlassen/Entlassung*
dot-com	*Internetunternehmen*
economics [iːkəˈnɒmɪks]	*Volkswirtschaft, Wirtschaftswissenschaft*
economist [ɪˈkɒnəmɪst]	*Volkswirt, Wirtschaftler*
enterprise	*Unternehmen, Betrieb, Gesellschaft*
equity [ˈɛkwɪti]	*Aktienkapital, Firmenkapital, Eigenkapital*
expansion	*Ausweitung, Erweiterung*
expenditure [ɪkˈspɛndɪtʃə]	*Kostenaufwand, Geldausgabe*
expertise [ˌɛkspəːˈtiːz]	*Gutachten*
fiscal	*finanz-, finanzwirtschaftlich, steuerrechtlich*
to franchise/franchise/franchising [ˈfran(t)ʃʌɪz]	*Lizenzvergabe/einen Lizenzvertrag haben*
GDP (*abbr.*, gross domestic product) [dʒiː diː ˈpiː]	*Bruttoinlandsprodukt*
holding	*Beteiligungsgesellschaft*
incentive	*Leistungsanreiz, Bonus, Bonuszahlung*
to incorporate/incorporated	*gründen, als Aktiengesellschaft eintragen/amtlich als AG eingetragen*
inflation	*Abwertung, Geldentwertung*
invoice	*Rechnung*
to lease/lease/leasing	*mieten, pachten/Mietvertrag, Pachtverhältnis*
liability/liable [lʌɪəˈbɪlɪti, ˈlʌɪəb(ə)l]	*Haftung, Haftungsbedingungen/haftbar*
liquidity [lɪˈkwɪdɪti]	*Zahlungsfähigkeit, Solvenz*

managerial [manə'dʒiːrɪəl]	*betriebswirtschaftlich, innerbetrieblich*
margin ['mɑːdʒɪn]	*Handelsspanne, Gewinnspanne*
memo/memorandum	*Aktennotiz, Gesprächsnotiz, Vermerk*
to merge/merger	*fusionieren/Unternehmensfusion*
monetary ['mʌnɪt(ə)ri]	*finanziell*
monopoly [mə'nɒp(ə)li]	*Monopol*
mortgage ['mɔːgɪdʒ]	*Hypothek*
to negotiate/negotiation [nɪ'gəʊʃɪeɪt, nɪgəʊʃɪ'eɪʃ(ə)n]	*verhandeln/Verhandlung*
operational/operator	*betriebsbedingt, betriebswirtschaftlich/Verkäufer*
organisational	*organisationsbedingt*
payable	*fällig sein, auszahlbar*
PC (*abbr.*, personal computer)	*Personalcomputer*
personnel [pəːsə'nɛl]	*Belegschaft, Mitarbeiter*
portfolio	*Resort, Geschäftsbereich*
privatization ['prʌɪvətʌɪ'zeɪʃ(ə)n]	*Privatisierung*
probability [prɒbə'bɪlɪti]	*Wahrscheinlichkeit*
profit/profitable	*Gewinn/ertragbringend, profitabel*
to purchase/purchaser ['pəːtʃɪs, 'pəːtʃɪsə(r)]	*kaufen, erwerben/Käufer*
recession	*Konjunkturrückgang, Konjunkturschwäche*
to regulate/regulatory	*etw. lenken, reglementieren/regelnd, regulatorisch*
to repay/repayment	*etw. abzahlen, tilgen/Abzahlung, Tilgung*
retail/retailing/retailer	*Einzelhandel/Einzelhändler*
revenue ['rɛvənjuː]	*Ertrag, Gewinn, Betriebseinkommen*

shareholder	*Aktionär, Anteilseigner*
start-up	*Existenzgründung*
statutory ['statjʊt(ə)ri]	*gesetzlich festgelegt, satzungsgemäß*
to subscribe/subscriber [səb'skrʌɪb, səb'skrʌɪbə(r)]	*etw. abonnieren/Abonnent*
subscription [səb'skrɪpʃ(ə)n]	*Abonnement*
subsidy/subsidiary *(adj.)* ['sʌbsɪdi, səb'sɪdɪəri]	*Zuschuss, Subvention/unterstützend*
subsidiary *(n.)* [səb'sɪdɪəri]	*Tochterfirma, Tochtergesellschaft, Nebenstelle*
to supply/supplier [sə'plʌɪ]	*beliefern/Lieferant*
takeover	*Firmenübernahme*
transaction	*Abwicklung/Abschluss eines Geschäftes*
turnover	*Gesamtumsatz, Geschäftsumsatz*
valuation	*Bewertung*
VAT (*abbr.*, value-added tax) [viː eɪ 'tiː, vat]	*Wertschöpfungsabgabe, Mehrwertsteuer*
vendor	*Verkäufer, Anbieter*
warranty ['wɒr(ə)nti]	*Garantie, Gewährleistung*
workforce	*Arbeiterschaft, Belegschaft*

Science & Technology

agricultural/agriculture [agrɪ'kʌltʃərəl]	*landwirtschaftlich/Landwirtschaft*
antibody ['antɪbɒdi]	*Antikörper, Immunkörper*
atomic [ə'tɒmɪk]	*atomar*
attribute [ə'trɪbjuːt]	*Eigenschaft, Kennzeichen, Merkmal*
binary (code/system) ['bʌɪnəri]	*binär, zweistellig*
biological [bʌɪə(ʊ)'lɒdʒɪk(ə)l]	*biologisch*
capability [keɪpə'bɪlɪti]	*Fähigkeit, Potential*
carbon/carbon dioxide ['kɑːb(ə)n dʌɪ'ɒksʌɪd]	*Kohlenstoff/Kohlendioxyd*
chromosome	*Chromosom*
chronic	*chronisch*
circuit ['səːkɪt]	*elektrisches System*
classification/to classify	*Eingruppierung, Klassifikation/ einstufen, eingruppieren*
to clone/clone/cloning	*klonen/Klon, Nachbau/Klonierung*
cluster	*Häufung, Anhäufung, Ballung*
component [kəm'pəʊnənt]	*Bestandteil, Bauteil*
compound ['kɒmpaʊnd]	*Stoff, chemische Verbindung, Gemisch*
to compute/computing	*etw. kalkulieren, einen Computer benutzen/EDV*
conservation	*Schutz, Umweltschutz, Naturschutz*
consistent [kən'sɪst(ə)nt]	*gleichartig, übereinstimmend*
to coordinate/coordinate [kəʊ'ɔːdɪneɪt]	*etw. abstimmen, koordinieren/ Koordinate*
crystal ['krɪst(ə)l]	*Kristall, Quarz*
database ['deɪtəbeɪs]	*Datenbank, Datenbestand*
density ['dɛnsɪti]	*Dichte, spezifisches Gewicht*

to detect	*etw. erkennen, ermitteln, feststellen, erfassen*
diagnosis [ˌdʌɪəg'nəʊsɪs]	*Diagnose*
diameter [dʌɪ'amɪtə]	*Durchmesser*
digit ['dɪdʒɪt]	*Ziffer*
digital ['dɪdʒɪt(ə)l]	*digital*
dimension [dɪ'mɛnʃ(ə)n, dʌɪ-]	*Ausmaß, Abmessung, Dimension*
to discharge/discharge	*etw. ableiten, entsorgen/Ableitung, Entsorgung*
DNA (*abbr.*, deoxyribonucleic acid) [diː ɛn 'eɪ]	*Desoxyribonukleinsäure (DNS)*
domain	*Arbeitsgebiet, Definitionsbereich*
dose	*Dosis, Dosierung, Portion*
electron	*Elektron*
to eliminate/elimination [ɪ'lɪmɪneɪt, ɪ'lɪmɪ'neɪʃ(ə)n]	*beseitigen, ausschließen/Ausschaltung, Beseitigung*
embryo ['ɛmbrɪəʊ]	*Embryo*
emission	*Ausstoß, Aussonderung*
enzyme ['ɛnzʌɪm]	*Enzym*
equation [ɪ'kweɪʒ(ə)n]	*(mathematische) Gleichung*
equilibrium [ţiːkwi 'lɪbrɪəm]	*Gleichgewicht*
evolution/evolutionary	*Entwicklung, Evolution/evolutionär*
experimental [ɪkˌspɛrɪ'mɛnt(ə)l]	*experimental, experimentell*
fibre ['fʌɪbə]	*Faser, Faserstoff*
fluid ['fluːɪd]	*Flüssigkeit*
fossil ['fɒs(ə)l]	*Fossil, Versteinerung*
fraction/fractions	*Bruchteil/Bruchrechnung*
gene [dʒiːn]	*Gen, Erbfaktor*
genetic/genetically/genetics [dʒɪ'nɛtɪk]	*genetisch, gentechnisch/Genetik*

gravity/gravitational ['gravɪti, gravɪ'teɪʃ(ə)nl]	*Schwerkraft/Gravitations-*
habitat ['habɪtat]	*Habitat, Lebensraum, Biotop*
hypothesis [hʌɪ'pɒθɪsɪs]	*Hypothese*
identical [ʌɪ'dɛntɪk(ə)l]	*identisch*
ion ['ʌɪən]	*Ion*
laser ['leɪzə]	*Laser*
magnetic [mag'nɛtɪk]	*magnetisch*
mammal ['mam(ə)l]	*Säugetier*
matrix ['meɪtrɪks]	*Matrix, Grundgerüst*
mechanical [mɪ'kanɪk(ə)l]	*mechanisch*
mechanics [mɪ'kanɪks]	*Mechanik, Mechanismus*
membrane ['mɛmbreɪn]	*Membran*
modification/to modify	*Abwandlung, Veränderung/ verändern, abwandeln*
molecular/molecule [mə'lɛkjʊlə]	*molekular/Molekül*
mutant/mutation ['mjuːt(ə)nt , mjuː'teɪʃ(ə)n]	*Mutation, Variante*
neutron ['njuːtrɒn]	*Neutron*
nuclear (energy) ['njuːklɪə]	*nuklear-, Kernenergie, Atomenergie*
nucleus ['njuːklɪəs]	*Atomkern, Zellkern, Kern*
organic	*kohlenstoffhaltig, organisch, biologisch-dynamisch*
organism	*Organismus*
oxygen ['ɒksɪdʒ(ə)n]	*Sauerstoff*
ozone (layer) ['əʊzəʊn]	*Ozon(-schicht)*
percentage [pə'sɛntɪdʒ]	*Prozent, Prozentanteil*
phenomenon [fɪ'nɒmɪnən]	*Phänomen*
radiation [reɪdɪ'eɪʃ(ə)n]	*(radioaktive, UV-) Strahlung, Bestrahlung*

research/researcher	*Forschung/Forscher*
satellite	*Satellit*
sequence/sequencing	*Ablauf, Aneinanderreihung/ Sequenzierung*
solar (energy)	*Sonnen-, Sonnenenergie*
species ['spiːʃiːz]	*Art, Gattung, Sorte*
to specify/specification ['spɛsɪfʌɪ, ˌspɛsɪfɪ'keɪʃ(ə)n]	*bestimmen, festlegen/Beschreibung, Festlegung*
statistics/statistical	*Statistik/statistisch*
stem (cell)	*Stamm(-zelle)*
symptom [sɪm(p)təm]	*Symptom, Merkmal*
transmission	*(Kraft-)Übertragung*
variable ['vɛːrɪəb(ə)l]	*unbeständig, wechselhaft, veränderlich*
vegetation [vɛdʒɪ'teɪʃ(ə)n]	*Vegetation, Pflanzenbestand*
wildlife	*Tier- und Pflanzenwelt, wildlebende Tiere*

Information Technology

aerial ['ɛːrɪəl]	*Antenne*
antenna	*Antenne*
application	*Anwendung, Anwendungsprogramm*
backslash	*Backslash (Schrägstrich von links oben nach rechts unten \ )*
bar code	*Strichcode*
blu-ray disc	*Blu-Ray-Disc*
Bluetooth	*Bluetooth (Industriestandard für die Funkvernetzung von Geräten über kurze Distanzen, um Kabelverbindungen zu ersetzen)*
button	*Taste*
cable television	*Kabelfernseher, Kabelempfang*
to capture sth.	*etw. einfangen, aufnehmen*
cloud computing	*Cloud Computing, Cloud IT, Rechnerwolke*
to come up (came up, came up)	*erscheinen*
to crash/crash	*abstürzen/Absturz*
data/database ['deɪtə, 'deɪtəbeɪs]	*Daten/Datenbank*
data processing	*Datenverarbeitung*
digital	*digital*
electrical/electronic/electronics	*elektrisch/elektronisch/Eletronik*
engineer/engineering	*Ingenieur/Technik/Ingenieurwissenschaft*
escape	*Escape-Taste*
to exit (a programme)	*ein Programm verlassen*
facility [fə'sɪlɪti]	*Funktion*
file extension [fʌɪl ɪk'stɛnʃ(ə)n]	*Dateierweiterung (z. B. .doc, .exe, .pdf etc.)*

graphics (program)	*Grafik(-programm)*
hardware	*Computer-Hardware (Rechner, Monitor, Drucker etc.)*
hyperlink/link [ˈhʌɪpəlɪŋk]	*Hyperlink, Link*
instructions	*Gebrauchsanweisung, Anleitung*
intercom	*Wechselsprechanlage*
intranet	*Intranet (unternehmensinternes Computer-Netzwerk)*
information technology (IT) [ˌaɪ tiː]	*Informationstechnik, Computertechnik*
input	*Dateneingabe*
key	*Taste*
keyboard	*Tastatur*
laboratory [ləˈbɒrəˌt(ə)ri]	*Laboratorium, Labor*
to launch [lɔːn(t)ʃ]	*in Betrieb nehmen, auf den Markt bringen*
local area network (LAN)	*lokales Netzwerk*
mainframe	*Großrechner*
memory	*(Daten-)Speicher*
memory card	*Speicherkarte*
meter	*Messgerät*
microprocessor [mʌɪkrə(ʊ)ˈprəʊsɛsə]	*Mikroprozessor*
mouse button	*Maustaste*
mouse mat/mouse pad	*Mauspad*
operating system (OS)	*Betriebssystem*
output	*Datenausgabe*
performance	*Leistung*
to process	*bearbeiten, verarbeiten*
process	*Verfahren*

programming	*programmieren*
to provide sth.	*etw. zur Verfügung stellen*
provider	*Dienstleister*
random access memory (RAM) [ræm]	*Arbeitsspeicher*
read only memory (ROM)	*Nur-Lese-Speicher*
satellite television ['satəlʌɪt]	*Satellitenfernsehen, Satellitenempfang*
server	*Netzwerkcomputer*
slash	*Schrägstrich (/)*
software	*Software (Computerprogramme)*
spreadsheet [sprɛd ʃiːt]	*Tabellenkalkulation*
to store	*speichern, sichern*
to switch off/on	*ausschalten/einschalten*
technology/technical/technique	*Technologie/technisch/Methode, Verfahren*
telecommunications [ˌtɛlɪkəmjuːnɪ'keɪʃ(ə)ns]	*Telekommunikation*
teletext	*Videotext*
text message	*SMS*
trial run ['trʌɪəl rʌn]	*Testreihe*
uniform resource locator (URL)	*URL (indivisuelle Internetadresse)*
to upload	*hinaufladen, kopieren*
WWW (World Wide Web)	*World Wide Web, Internet*
(web) browser	*Browser, Internetnavigationsprogramm*
wireless local area network (WLAN)	*drahtloses lokales Netzwerk*
to zip	*(eine Datei) komprimieren*

Education & Social Affairs

(sexual) abuse	*(sexueller) Missbrauch*
advanced	*fortgeschritten, Fortgeschrittenen-*
affair	*Affäre, Seitensprung*
affairs	*private Angelegenheiten, Privatleben*
age group	*Altersgruppe*
aid	*Hilfe, Unterstützung*
antisocial	*unsozial, antisozial*
attendance	*Anwesenheit, Schulbesuch*
bachelor	*Junggeselle*
to break up (broke up, broke up) *(phr. v.)*	*auseinandergehen*
care	*Fürsorge, Obhut*
charity	*Wohlfahrtsverband*
(to do the) chores [tʃɔːs]	*(die) Hausarbeit (erledigen)*
conduct	*Benehmen, Verhalten*
to contribute/contribution [kənˈtrɪbjuːt, kɒntrɪˈbjuːʃ(ə)n]	*helfen, unterstützen/Hilfe, Unterstützung*
counsellor [ˈkaʊns(ə)lə]	*berufsmäßige(r) Berater(in) in sozialen Fragen*
curriculum [kʌˈrɪkjʊləm]	*Lehrplan*
day care centre	*Kindertagesstätte*
(physically/mentally) disabled	*(körperlich oder geistig) behindert*
disability	*Behinderung*
learning disabilities	*Lernbehinderung(en)*
to discriminate/discrimination	*diskriminieren/Diskriminierung*
distance learning	*Fernunterricht*
divorce	*Ehescheidung*
educational background	*Ausbildung*

the elderly	*die ältere Generation*
to encourage/encouragement [ɪnˈkʌrɪdʒ, ɪnˈkʌrɪdʒm(ə)nt]	*ermutigen, unterstützen/Unterstützung, Förderung*
extended family	*Großfamilie*
family planning	*Familienplanung, Geburtenregelung*
family/social background	*Familienmilieu, soziale Herkunft*
full-time/part-time/flexitime	*Vollzeit-, Teilzeit-, Gleitzeit*
gap	*Konflikt, Lücke, Kluft*
generation gap [ˌdʒenəˈreɪʃn gæp]	*Generationenkonflikt*
to get by (got by got by)	*auskommen, zurechtkommen*
to give away (gave away given away)	*spenden*
homeless/homeless person/ homelessness	*obdachlos, Obdachlose(r)/ Obdachlosigkeit*
impaired/visually/hearing impaired	*körperlich eingeschränkt, geschädigt/sehbehindert/hörbehindert*
income	*Einkommen*
cooperative	*entgegenkommend, kooperativ*
the Labour Movement	*Arbeiterbewegung*
lifestyle	*Lebensstil*
to look after sb. *(phr. v.)*	*sich um jdn. kümmern*
middle class	*Mittelschicht*
minority	*Minderheit*
move in	*zusammenziehen, einziehen*
mutual [ˈmjuːtʃʊəl]	*gegenseitig, beiderseitig*
need	*Not, Bedürftigkeit, Bedürfnis*
nuclear family	*Kleinfamilie, bestehend z. B. aus Vater, Mutter und Kind*
nursery	*Kinderkrippe, Kinderhort*
nursery school/kindergarten	*Kindergarten, Vorschule*

old age pension	*Altersrente, Pension*
old people's home	*Seniorenheim, Altenheim*
to participate/participation	*sich beteiligen, teilnehmen/ Teilnahme, Teilhabe*
patchwork family	*Patchworkfamilie*
pensioner ['pɛnʃ(ə)nə]	*Rentner(in)*
the poverty line	*Armutsgrenze*
prejudice/prejudiced ['prɛdʒʊdɪs, 'prɛdʒədɪst]	*Vorurteil/voreingenommen*
private school	*Privatschule (mit Gebühren)*
(to enjoy a) privilege ['prɪvɪlɪdʒ]	*(ein/en) Privileg, Vorzug (genießen)*
relation/relative	*Verwandte(r)*
related	*verwandt*
retired/retiree [rɪ'tʌɪəd]	*pensioniert, im Ruhestand/ Pensionär, Ruheständler*
security	*Sicherheit, Geborgenheit*
senior citizen	*Senior(in), ältere(r) Bürger(in)*
share	*Anteil, Beitrag*
shelter	*Asyl, Einrichtung für sozial Benachteiligte*
single parent	*Alleinerziehende(r)*
skill	*Fähigkeit, Fertigkeit*
social change	*sozialer Wandel*
social class	*soziale Klasse/Schicht*
social security	*Sozialhilfe(-zahlung), staatliche Sozialversicherung*
social status ['steɪtəs]	*gesellschaftliche Stellung*
social worker	*Sozialarbeiter(in)*
(financial) support	*(finanzielle) Unterstützung*

state school (BE)/public school (US)	*staatliche/öffentliche Schule*
unmarried	*unverheiratet, alleinstehend*
upbringing	*(familiäre) Erziehung*
upper class	*Oberschicht*
vocational [və(ʊ)ˈkeɪʃ(ə)n(ə)l]	*berufsbezogen*
welfare	*soziale Fürsorge, Sozialhilfeleistung*
welfare state	*Wohlfahrtsstaat*
wheelchair accessible [əkˈsɛsɪb(ə)l]	*rollstuhlgerecht, mit dem Rollstuhl befahrbar*
a woman's shelter	*Frauenhaus*
the women's movement	*Frauenbewegung*
working class	*Arbeiterklasse*

Art & Design

abstract ['æbstrækt]	*Entwurf, abstraktes Gemälde*
aesthetic [iːs'θɛtɪk]	*ästhetisch, kunstvoll, geschmackvoll*
architect/architectural/architecture ['ɑːkɪtɛkt, 'ɑːkɪtɛktʃə]	*Architekt/architektonisch/ Architektur*
auction/auctioneer ['ɑːkʃ(ə)n, ɔːkʃə'nɪə]	*(Kunst-)Auktion/Auktionator*
bourgeois ['bʊəʒwɑː]	*bürgerlich*
brushstroke	*Pinselstrich, Pinselführung*
canvas	*Leinwand*
choreographer ['kɒrɪ'ɒgrəfə/]	*Choreograph*
classical	*klassisch*
to collect/collector	*sammeln/(Kunst-)Sammler*
to compose/composition	*komponieren/Komposition, Arrangement*
creative/creativity [kriː'eɪtɪv, ˌkriːeɪ'tɪvɪti]	*kreativ/Kreativität*
critic	*Kritiker*
dealer	*Händler*
distinctive	*unverkennbar, unverwechselbar*
dynamic [dʌɪ'namɪk]	*dynamisch, bewegt*
epoch ['iːpɒk, 'ɛpɒk]	*Epoche*
era ['ɪərə]	*Ära, Epoche, Zeitalter*
establishment	*Herstellung, Schaffung, das Establishment*
fiction/fictional	*erzählende Literatur, Prosa/ erfunden, fiktiv, erzählerisch*
fragment	*Bruchstück, Fragment, Bruchteil*
graphic/graphics	*anschaulich, detailliert dargestellt/ Grafik(en)*

historic	*historisch*
illustration	*Illustration, Veranschaulichung*
imagery/visual imagery ['ɪmɪdʒ(ə)ri]	*Metaphorik/Bildersymbolik*
imaginative [ɪ'madʒɪnətɪv]	*fantasievoll*
installation	*(künstlerische) Installation*
mainstream	*Hauptrichtung, der Mitte der Gesellschaft angehörend*
masterpiece	*Meisterwerk*
pastel ['past(ə)l]	*Pastellzeichnung*
to perceive/perception [pə'siːv, pə'sɛpʃ(ə)n]	*wahrnehmen/Wahrnehmung*
portrait/to portray sb./sth. ['pɔːtrɪt, pɔː'treɪ]	*Porträt/jdn. porträtieren*
profile ['prəʊfaɪl]	*Profilbild, Seitenansicht*
realism	*Realismus*
reflection of sth.	*Reflexion, Spiegelung, Widerspiegelung*
rehearsal [rɪ'həːs(ə)l]	*Probe*
revival	*Wiedererwecken, Wiederaufgreifen*
rhythmic ['rɪðmɪk]	*rhythmisch*
sculptor/sculpture ['skʌlptə, 'skʌlptʃə]	*Bildhauer/Plastik*
sketch/to sketch	*Skizze/skizzieren*
watercolour	*Aquarell*
workshop	*Werkstatt, Workshop*

The Function of Marketing and Marketing Instruments

Marketing is "the activity, set of institutions, and processes for creating, communicating, delivering, and exchanging offerings that have value for customers, clients, partners, and society at large" (American Marketing Association). In a wider context, marketing is the strategy that underlies **sales techniques, business communication and business development**. Focusing on the customer, marketing management is one of the major components of business management, aimed at **developing new markets** and **satisfying customer requirements profitably**. Based on the knowledge of the needs and wants of the **target consumers (market research)**, marketing concepts and strategies strive to satisfy consumers more effectively than competitors.

The function of marketing in a company

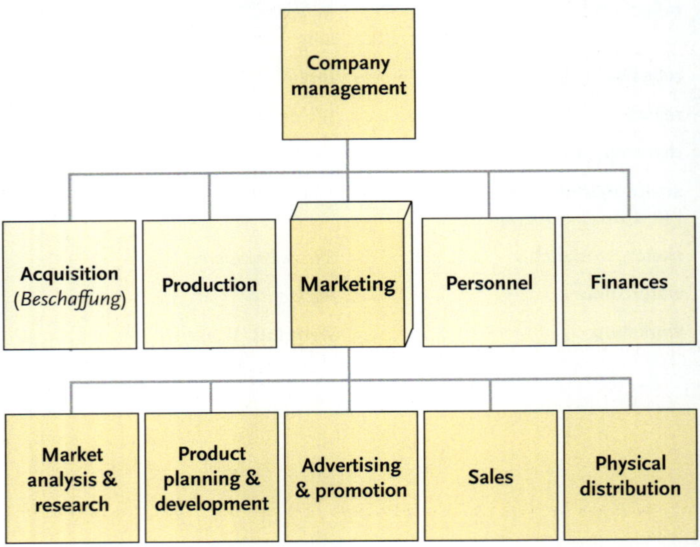

Marketing concepts and strategies

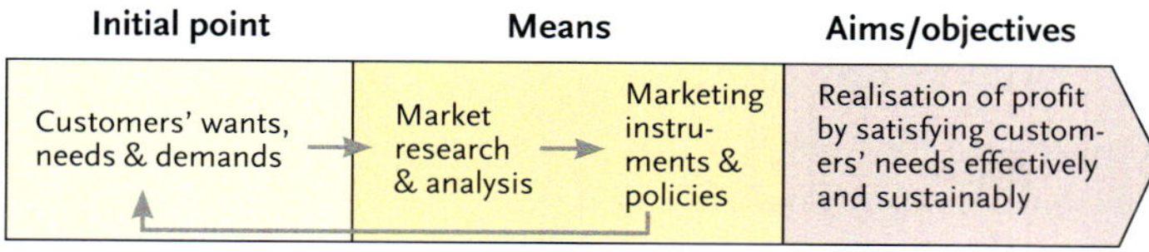

Marketing instruments and policies *(Methode, Strategie)*

product & service policy	**contracting policy**	**distribution policy**	**communication policy**
– quality – configuration – innovation – branding strategy – assortment (*Sortiment*) / range – services – warranties/liability (*Haftung*) – labelling (*Beschriftung*)	– pricing & discount – price-performance ratio (*Preis-Leistungs-Verhältnis*) – terms & conditions of delivery and payment	– method of distribution – organization – distribution channel (*Absatzkanal*) – logistics – delivery – transport	– advertising – direct marketing – sales promotion – buying behaviour: • business-to-business (B2B) • business-to-consumer (B2C) – public relations (PR) – sponsoring – event marketing
→ What is offered to the customers?	→ What are the precise conditions?	→ Where/How are the goods offered/distributed?	→ How is the contact to the customer established/maintained?

from *Marketing* by Hans Christian Weiß. Kiehl, Ludwigshafen 1982; translated by Iris Edelbrock

Factors of the Market Economy

The circular flow model

The circular flow model depicts the **workings of the economy and the movement of resources** between producers and consumers. There are various models, comprising[1] different flows:

- the flow comprising **wages and salaries** paid by the firms to the households → income
- the flow of money spent by **households** and received by **firms** → expenditure[2]
- the corresponding flow of **labour** provided by households to firms
- the flow of **goods and services** provided by firms to households.

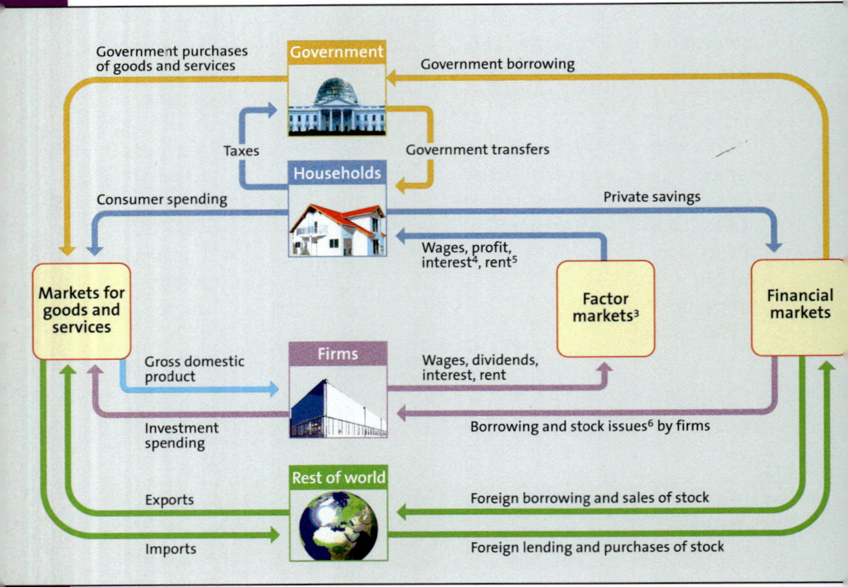

[1] **to comprise** *beinhalten* – [2] **expenditure** *Ausgaben* – [3] **factor market** *Produktionsmarkt* – [4] **interest** *Zinsen* – [5] **rent** *Miete* – [6] **stock issue** *Aktienausgabe*

Additionally, there are certain leakages from the flow: **savings** (when money is received by households but not spent), **imports** (where money flows to foreign firms) and **taxation** (when money flows to the government). In addition to these "withdrawals" there are certain inflows of money, i.e. investment, exports and government spending – which ideally balance each other out.

The "supply and demand" model of the market and its consequences

Supply and demand is an economic model of price determination in a market. There are **four basic laws**:

1. If demand increases and supply remains unchanged, then it leads to a higher price and production rises.
2. If demand decreases and supply remains unchanged, then it leads to a lower price and less is produced.
3. If supply increases and demand remains unchanged, then it leads to a lower price and production rises.
4. If supply decreases and demand remains unchanged, then it leads to a higher price and less is produced.

Consumer Protection and Protection Authorities

Consumer protection aims at ensuring the rights of consumers, fair trade, competition and the flow of reliable information in the marketplace. Consumer organizations have set up rules that

a) require businesses to give information about their products with regard to safety or public health.

b) help consumers with complaints, protect their rights and provide them with information.

Consumer protection is provided by government organizations, consumer protection agencies/organizations and non-governmental organizations.

Consumer protection law includes a wide range of activities, e. g.:

- product liability
- unfair business practices
- service and sales contracts
- competition regulation
- credit repair/debit repair
- pollution control/environmental protection
- fraud *(Betrug)*
- product safety
- pricing
- privacy rights

Germany

- a **minister of the federal cabinet** is responsible for consumer rights and protection (*Verbraucherschutzminister*)
- there is no specific law for consumer protection in Germany, but the **Civil Code of Germany** (*Bürgerliches Gesetzbuch/BGB*) is a codification of regulations that cover civil law, environmental issues, the German Commercial Code, etc.
- there are **several governmental and non-governmental institutions** and agencies that deal with Consumer rights, e. g.: Federal Ministry of Food, Agriculture and Consumer Protection; Federal Office of Consumer Protection and Food Safety; Federal Office for Agriculture and Food; Federation of German Consumer Organisations (*Verbraucherzentrale, vzbv*); *Stiftung Warentest*; etc.

United Kingdom

- the **Office of Fair Trading (OFT)** and its Director-General deal with consumer protection and complaints and act as the official consumer and competition watchdog
- until 2010, the government-funded call centre **Consumer Direct** provided consumer information
- since March 2012 the **Citizens Advice** consumer service has taken its place (www.adviceguide.org.uk)
- a set of parliamentary acts regulate consumer protection, e.g.: Consumer Credit Act (1974); Unfair Trade Terms Act (1977); Sales of Goods Act (1979); Consumer Protection Act (1987); Consumer Protection from Unfair Trading Regulations (2008); etc.
- important British **consumer advice organizations** are, e.g.: Citizens Advice Bureau; Office of Fair Trading; Advertising Standards Authority (ASA); Which?; etc.

USA

- the majority of US states have a **Department of Consumer Affairs** that regulates industries and protects consumer rights
- California has the strongest consumer protection laws of the US and the **California Department of Consumer Affairs** regulates about 2.3 million professionals/230 different professions
- on the federal level, consumer protection laws are enforced by the **Federal Trade Commission** (FTC) and the U.S. Department of Justice (www.ftc.gov/bcp/consumer.shtm)
- U.S. **consumer advice and advocacy organizations** are, e.g.: Consumer Action; Privacy Rights Clearinghouse; Utility Consumers' Action Network (UCAN); etc.
- some important governmental acts dealing with consumer protection are e.g.: Federal Meat Inspection Act (1906); Pure Food and Drug Act (1906); Federal Food, Drug and Cosmetic Act (1938); Poultry Products Inspection Act (1957); etc.

→ Further consumer rights institutions/agencies: Webcode SNG-40170-014 @

Trade Unions

A trade union is an organization of workers who have united to achieve common goals. The trade union negotiates e. g. labour contracts (= collective bargaining) with the employer on behalf of the union members with the purpose of maintaining or improving the conditions of their employment and work, e. g.:

- (higher) **wages**/pay
- **complaint** procedures
- **benefits**
- workplace **safety**
- work **rules**
- better **working conditions**
- increasing the **number of employees**
- **working hours**
- rules concerning **hiring, firing and/or promotion of workers**

Further objectives and activities are e. g.:

- benefits to **insure members** in case of unemployment, illness, retirement, etc. (most commonly practised in developing countries in which the state does not provide these services)
- provision of **professional training**
- enforcement of **strikes**
- organizing **political campaigns**
- **assistance to the government**
- **legal advice**
- **resistance** to lockouts by the employer
- **lobbying**

Origins

Trade unions became particularly popular in Europe during the **Industrial Revolution (ca. 1750–1859)** when the employment bargaining power shifted almost completely to the employers, thus causing a **growing imbalance of power** between employer and worker and leaving many **workers to be mistreated and underpaid**. Back then, **membership in a trade union was illegal** in most countries and there were severe penalties for organizing unions, in some cases even execution. **Today**, the right to join a trade union is stated in the **Universal Declaration of Human Rights** (Article 29) and prohibiting a person from joining or organizing a trade union is considered a human rights violation.

Unions in Europe – structure and politics

Germany: Socialist parties and democrats helped form and build up trade unions in the **19th century**, after the German Revolution of 1848. The most important organization is the **German Confederation of Trade Unions** (*Deutscher Gewerkschaftsbund*) with about 7 million organized people. The single largest trade union is the ***IG Metall*** (2.3 mio members) which organizes employees of the metal, electronics, steel, textile, wood and synthetics industries.
In Germany, the employees' representation has a **binary structure**:

a) **Trade unions** negotiate working conditions, collective wage agreements and define wage levels and working time for whole sectors or single companies.
b) **Works councils** (*Betriebsräte*) are elected by the employees and represent their interests on the company level.

In so-called "companies boards" (*Aufsichtsrat*) trade unionists and works councils have full voting rights and a high degree of co-determination.

United Kingdom: Historically and politically, **trade unionism** was stronger than the political labour movement which even opposed trade unionism.
In the economic crises of the 1960s/70s, ca. 12 mio workers in the UK were trade union members who organized significant strikes. At the peak of the strikes, nearly 30 mio working days were lost during 1979. That year, a trade union reform led by the newly elected Conservative Party (Margaret Thatcher) caused a severe drop in the level of strikes and union members to ca. 6 mio in the late 1980s.
Since the **end of the Cold War** in 1989 unionization in many eastern European countries has collapsed (e.g. the Solidarity Union from 9.5 mio members in 1981 to 400,000 in 2010). Today only 1/4 of the people employed in the EU are members of a trade union: Italy 30 %, UK 29 %, Germany 27 % and France 9 %.

→ List of Trade Unions worldwide: Webcode SNG-40170-015 @

The Challenge of Demographic Change

The increase in life span and the global development of dementia

Since modern ***Homo sapiens* first appeared in the world at around 50,000 B.C.**, an estimated total of 108 billion people have lived on earth – which means that about **6.5 % of all humans ever born are alive today**. The problem of feeding and sustaining a population that size is that the **resources are not always where the people are**. Consequently, the challenge for the future will be to make sure that people, especially in poorer regions, get **access to food, health care, education**, etc. Governments are focusing on maintaining productive and effective economies in order to be able to take care of the **rising number of elderly people** and the problems connected with it, coping with shortages of fossil fuel and tackling the still unsolved problem of extreme poverty in many regions of the world.

Population by age and sex

There were 12 working-age people for every person over 65 in 1950; by 2050 there will be 3.

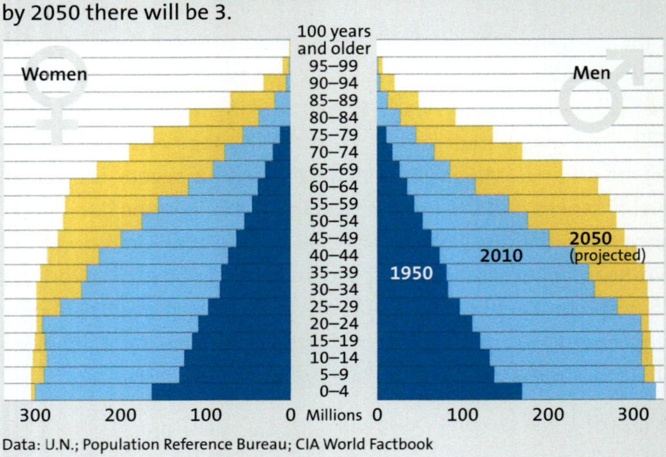

Data: U.N.; Population Reference Bureau; CIA World Factbook

By 2050, the number of people suffering from dementia will triple to 115 million. The increase will be particularly dramatic in developing countries due to the rising life expectancy there. About 4.7% of people aged 60 suffer from dementia.

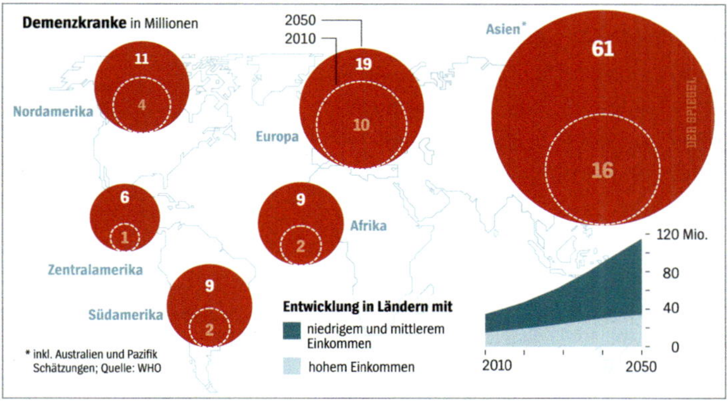

The global fertility rate

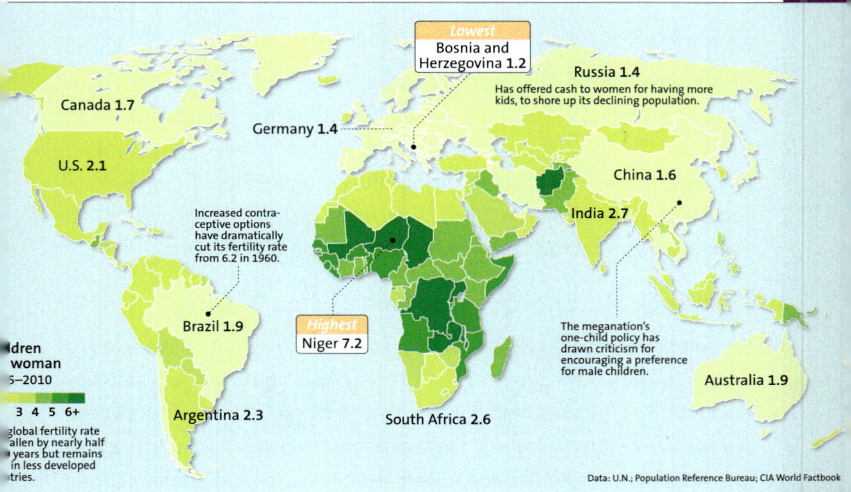

Human Needs

Abraham Maslow: "The Hierarchy of Human Needs"

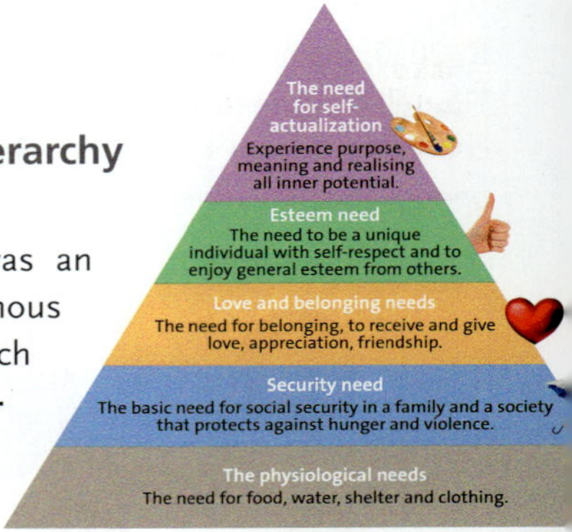

Abraham Maslow(1908–1970) was an American psychologist most famous for his model of human needs which he published in 1943. Maslow **classified our needs under five headings** and put them in a hierarchy – the order in which he believed we satisfy them. He said that we use our energy first to find food and drink. If we have energy left, we then use it to defend our sources of food and drink. When means of satisfying these basic needs are established and secured, we make friends, seek recognition and become independent and autonomous. This **was the order in which he placed them**:

1. physiological or basic needs
2. security or safety needs
3. social or belonging needs
4. status or ego or esteem[1] needs
5. self-fulfilment or self-actualization needs

The **higher needs are enjoyed in the mind**. Belonging and status needs can be satisfied fully. But self-fulfilment is insatiable[2] – we can never fully satisfy it. It is our highest level of need and it seems to feed off itself. **We can apply Maslow's hierarchy of needs to all people at work**, whether male or female, young or old, or whether they work in a factory, office or the executive boardroom.

Frederick Herzberg: "The Two Factor Theory"

Frederick Herzberg (1923–2000) was an American psychologist who was most famous for his "Two Factor Theory" of job satisfaction (1959). He published his findings in the 1959 book *The Motivation of Work*. The following table presents the **top six factors causing** satisfaction **and the top seven factors causing dissatisfaction**.

Relevant factors leading to satisfaction/motivators/ satisfiers	**Importance**	**Relevant factors leading to dissatisfaction/hygiene[3] factors**
• achievement • recognition • work itself • responsibility • advancement • growth	**High** **Importance** **Low**	• company policy • supervision • relationship with boss • work conditions • salary • relationship with peers • security

Herzberg's researchers interviewed two hundred white- and blue-collar employees (accountants and engineers) and recorded 1,753 incidents that interviewers claimed made them feel good about their work.

Then they gathered 1,844 incidents that made people dissatisfied. **Herzberg showed that the factors which cause dissatisfaction are different from those which cause satisfaction**. They are not just the negatives of the latter. If these satisfiers and hygiene factors are put **alongside Maslow's model**, it becomes apparent that the **hygiene factors equate to the lower needs, whilst the satisfiers equate to the higher needs**. So it can be deduced that if lower needs are not adequately met, workers will be dissatisfied. If they are adequately met, people will not be dissatisfied.

If people's lower needs are met at work, they will not be dissatisfied with their jobs. If, in addition, their higher needs are met, they will be satisfied with their jobs. **It is necessary to meet both lower and higher needs to ensure people enjoy job satisfaction.**

from *People, Marketing & Business* by Malcolm Surridge et al. Collins Educational, London 1993, pp. 16 ff.

---

[1] **esteem** *Ansehen, Hochachtung* – [2] **insatiable** [ɪn'seɪʃəbl] *unersättlich* – [3] **hygiene** ['haɪdʒiːn]

Immigration and Minorities in the United States

The English went to North America from the late 16th century; Spain sent people to the southern part of the region and many Dutch and Germans also went over. When the U. S. became independent, it was written into the **Constitution** that there could be no limits on immigration until 1808. The main period of immigration was between 1800 and 1917. Early in this period, many more immigrants arrived from Britain and Germany, and many Chinese went to California. Later, the main groups were Italians, Irish, Eastern Europeans and Scandinavians. Many Jews came from Germany and Eastern Europe. Just before World War I, there were nearly a million immigrants a year. Most Americans have a clear idea of what life was like for the immigrants: they left home because they were poor and thought they would have better opportunities in the U. S. Many immigrants came to New York and Boston, and **Ellis Island**, near New York, became famous as a receiving station.

The **Immigration Act of 1917**, and other laws that followed it, limited the number of immigrants who could settle in the U. S. and the countries that they could come from. Since then, immigration has been limited to a few people who are selected for an **immigrant visa**, commonly called a green card. Hispanics and Asians now make up the largest groups of immigrants. **The Immigration and Naturalization Service** (INS) is responsible for issuing visas. It also tries to prevent people from crossing the borders and entering the U. S. illegally.

Ethnic minorities in the USA (US census of 2010)

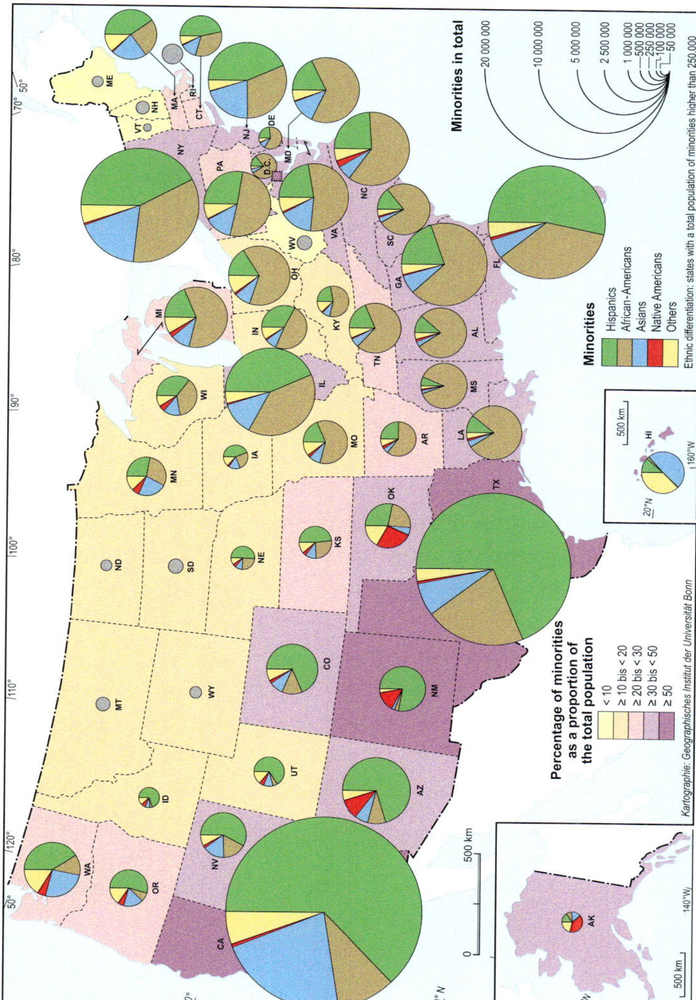

Great Britain – A Multicultural Society

Immigration and minorities in Great Britain

People have been coming to Britain for centuries, but immigration only became an issue in the 1960s.
After World War II, Britain needed more workers and admitted citizens of Commonwealth countries without restriction. Many came from the Caribbean and from India, Pakistan and Bangladesh. They found work in hospitals, in the textile industry and in the public transport system, though most jobs were poorly paid. **Nearly 500,000 Commonwealth citizens came to Britain before 1962**, many of whom were later joined by their families. When there were no longer enough jobs, **the Commonwealth Immigrants Act (1962)** was passed to restrict the number of immigrants entering Britain. In the following years, several more acts were passed, further restricting the right of foreigners to live in Britain. **Immigration is now strictly controlled**. Normally, only people from the European Union and certain Commonwealth citizens can get permission to live in Britain. Britain now accepts about 50,000 immigrants every year.
After periods of racism and violent demonstrations in the 1960s and 1970s, Britain has been making great efforts to integrate people from ethnic minorities into local communities and to develop a multicultural society based on equality and acceptance.

Statistical data about minorities and population trends in Britain

The country of origin of people living in Great Britain, 2001 (%)

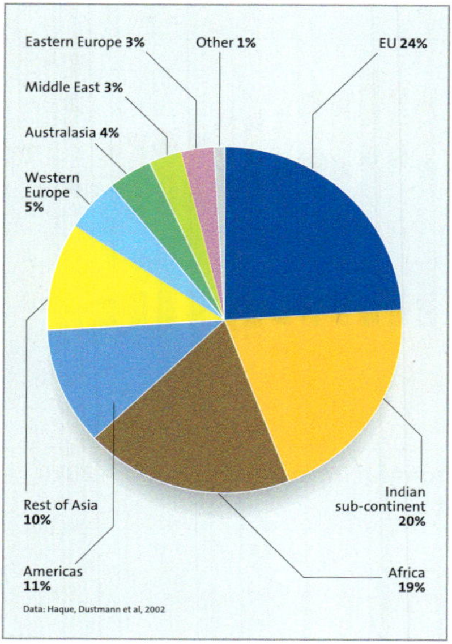

The non-white population of Great Britain, 1951–2001

Year	Non-white population
1951	30,000 (est.)
1961	400,000 (est.)
1971	1.4 million
1981	2.1 million
1991	3.0 million
2001	4.6 million

Data: for 1951 and 1961, Spencer (1997); for 1971, Lornas (1973); for 1981, Amin & Richardson (1992); for 1991 and 2001, Office for National Statistics and General Register Office for Scotland

Further data on the EU population and foreign-born European citizens as of 2010/2011 can be found on links provided on the webcode.

Webcode SNG-40170-021 @

Migration and immigration control

The British Office for National Statistics releases a **quarterly summary of the official migration data**. It reveals information about the reasons why people apply for residence in the United Kingdom.

Migrant applications for work in the UK, 2004–2010

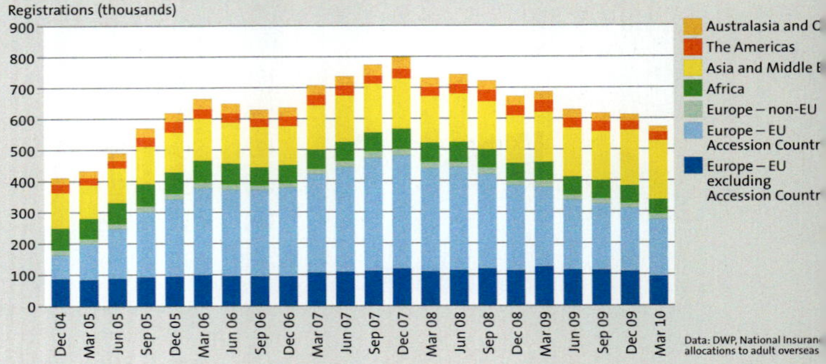

Data: DWP, National Insuran allocations to adult overseas

UK entry visas issued by reasons for intended entry, 2005–2010

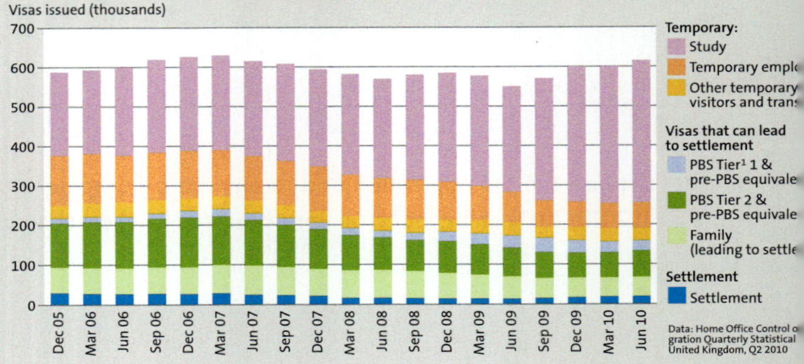

Data: Home Office Control o gration Quarterly Statistical United Kingdom, Q2 2010

---

[1] **tier** [tɪə(r)] level

In order to control and systematize immigration there are several visa categories:

- the visitor and transit visa
- **The Points Based System (PBS):**
  - PBS Tier 1: highly skilled workers
  - PBS Tier 2: skilled workers with a job offer
  - PBS Tier 3: low skilled workers
  - PBS Tier 4: students
  - PBS Tier 5: youth mobility and temporary workers

  The PBS, implemented in 2008, is a rationalization of immigration control processes for people who are not citizens of the European Economic Area (EEA) or Swiss nationals.

The Industrial Revolution

The **Industrial Revolution in England** established **the economic pattern of the modern world**. The (first) Industrial Revolution took place in Britain (~1760–1830) and marked the **change from an agrarian, handicraft economy to industry and machine production**, whereas the **second Industrial Revolution** (late 19th and 20th centuries) was based on modern industry, the exploitation of natural and synthetic resources and new energy resources as well as new machines, tools and computers which facilitated automatic operation and production. Additionally, there was a new understanding of ownership though the purchase of stocks instead of owning the means of production.

Causes

- Britain has a range of **natural ports facing the Atlantic Ocean** and utilizes coastal shipping.
- Britain has a good system of internal waterways and canals.
- **Britain's colonies** provide raw materials and customers for manufactured goods.
- **1775 James Watt invents the steam engine** which revolutionizes the (industrial) production of steel, cotton, mining, etc.

Main features, core components and technological changes

- the use of **new basic materials**, e.g. iron and steel
- the use of **new inanimate sources of energy** (instead of human or animal power), including fuels and motive power: coal, water (the steam engine), electricity, petroleum (the internal combustion engine)
- the **invention of new machines**, e.g. the power loom
  → increased production; less human energy, lower costs
- the **factory system**, i.e. increased division/specialization of labour
- **developments in transportation/communication**

- increasing **application of science** to industry
- **agrarian revolution**: new crop rotation system; closed field system (enclosures); improvement in livestock breeding

Changes and impacts

- increased use and **exploitation of natural resources**
- **mass production** of manufactured goods
- **exploitation of workers** (e. g. child labour) and suffering farmers cause poverty and misery
- **economic changes**, e. g. unequal distribution of wealth; social imbalances between rich and poor
- **increased international trade**
- **political changes**
- **major social changes**, e. g. urbanization
- **cultural transformations**:
  - man becomes a 'machine operator' (instead of a craftsman) and is subject to factory discipline
  - **concentration of workers in enterprises** (factory system); new authority: the entrepreneur
  - decision-making not by prescriptive authorities (king, priest) but 'experts'
- **free labour market** instead of old feudal ties
- **demographic changes**:
  - during the 18th century: population growth in Europe: 100 mio → 200 mio
  - during the 19th century: population growth in Europe: 200 mio → 400 mio
- **urbanization**:
  - 1801: 20 % of UK population lives in towns and cities of 10,000 or more inhabitants
  - 1901: 75 % of UK population lives in towns and cities of 10,000 or more inhabitants
    50 % of UK population lives in towns and cities of 20,000 or more inhabitants

Genetic Engineering

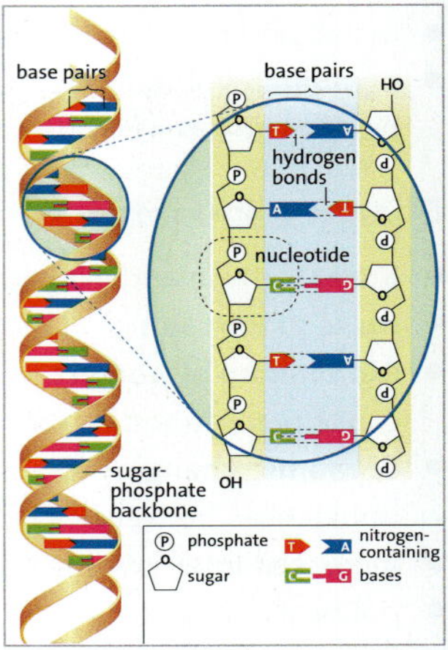

Genetic engineering (or genetic modification) is the **human manipulation of an organism's genetic material** to create a genetically modified organism that does not exist under natural conditions. During this process, new genetic material (DNA) is inserted into the host genome (= the entirety of an organism's hereditary information). First the **genetic material of interest is isolated and copied**, thereby generating a construct that contains all the necessary genetic elements, which is then **inserted into a host organism** in a second step.

Thus, **genetic engineering changes the genetic design or genetic blueprint of an organism** and **forms new combinations** of heritable (= *erblich*) genetic material. Although **stem cell research** and **cloning** are not considered to be genetic engineering by definition, these areas of scientific research are closely connected to genetic engineering because they can be used together.

In **medicine** genetic engineering is used e.g. for **the mass production of insulin, human growth hormones, follitism (for treating infertility) and vaccines**. Researchers are also working to genetically engineer humans and e.g. **replace defective humans genes with functional ones** and thus **cure genetic disorders and diseases** like Parkinson's disease, cancer, diabetes, heart diseases and arthritis. Despite all the (possible) benefits of genetic engineering there are also **ethical concerns and criticism** that this technology is not only used for treatment but for enhancement, modification or alteration of a human being's character, behaviour, appearance, intelligence or adaptability.

Historical development

Year	Major scientific discovery or achievement
1856–1863	Austrian monk and scientist **Gregor Johann Mendel** (1822–1884) shows that the inheritance of certain traits follows particular laws (the **"Laws of Inheritance"**); he is considered to be the "father of modern genetics"
1953	American zoologist **James Watson** and British physicist **Francis Crick discover the double helix**, the chemical structure of DNA which makes up genes
1972	American biochemist **Paul Berg creates the first recombinant** (= altered, modified) **DNA**
1974	German biologist **Rudolf Jaenisch creates a transgenic mouse** by inserting foreign DNA into its embryo
1976	Genetic Engineering Technology Inc. (Genentech Inc.), **the first biotechnology company, is founded in California** by US businessman Robert A. Swanson and biochemist Dr. Herbert Boyer
1978	Genentech Inc. **produces genetically engineered human insulin**
1980	the **US Supreme Court rules that genetically altered life can be patented**
1986	first field trials in the **USA and France: genetically engineered tobacco plants** are resistant to herbicides (= *Unkrautvernichtungsmittel*)
1992	**China commercializes virus-resistant tobacco plants**
1994	the **first genetically-modified tomato**, designed to have a longer shell life, is released
June 2000	President Clinton announces **the completion of the first draft of the human genome**
Feb 2001	first analyses of the public and private genome projects are published; the big discovery: **Humans have about 30,000 to 40,000 genes, hardly more than a common weed or worm**
April 2003	the **human genome is declared a finished product**; the announcement coincides with the 50th anniversary of the discovery of the double helix

The European Union

The European Union (EU) is an **economic and political union** of 27 member states (ca. 500 million citizens) that has developed a single market **ensuring free movement of people, goods, services and capital**. The EU operates through supranational and intergovernmental negotiations and treaties between the member states. Economically the EU generates ca. 20 % of the gross world product.

History

1957	**Rome Treaty** creates the European Economic Community (EEC) as a customs union members: Belgium, France, Italy, Luxembourg, the Netherlands, West Germany
1979	first direct democratic elections to the **European Parliament**
1985	**Schengen Agreement** creates open borders without passport control between most member states
1986	the European flag is first used
1990	after German reunification, (former) East Germany joins the community
1993	in the **Maastricht Treaty**, the European Union is formally established
2002	the **Euro** is introduced as European currency and replaces national currencies in twelve of the member states

Fundamental rights

- In 2009, the **Lisbon Treaty** gave legal effect to the **Charter of Fundamental Rights of the European Union** which is a catalogue of fundamental (human) rights which were derived from the constitutional traditions of the member states (e. g. **Article 1:** Human dignity is inviolable. It must be respected and protected; **Article 2:** Everyone has the right to life. No one shall be condemned to the death penalty, or executed.).

Important EU institutions

- the **European Council** is the EU's supreme political authority; it defines the EU's political agenda and strategies
- the **European Commission** is the EU's executive branch and responsible for its legislation
- the **European Parliament** (in Strasbourg) forms half of the EU's legislature; the members of the European Parliament are directly elected by the EU citizens every five years
- the **Council of the European Union** is the other half of the EU's legislature; in addition to legislative functions it also has executive functions, e. g. the Common Foreign and Security Policy
- the **Court of Justice of the European Union** interprets and applies the treaties and the law of the EU
- the **European Central Bank** administers the monetary policy of the 16 member states taking part in the **Eurozone**; it is one of the world's most important central banks

The 27 EU member states

Global Economy

Historical roots

- **early "world economies"** like **Phoenicia** (1200–800 B.C.), the **Roman Empire** (510 B.C. – 500 A.D.), the **Silk Road** (1st century) and the **British East India Company** (founded in 1608) establish an international network of trading routes and found commercial outposts
- **inventions and discoveries** of the late **Middle Ages** and **Renaissance** enable people **in Europe** to sail and **travel longer distances** and become less dependable on weather conditions (e.g. 13th cent.: magnetic compass, mechanical clock, spectacles/lenses, scales for weighing; 16th/17th cent.: pocket watch, thermometer, telescope) ➔ international trading and exchange of goods is fostered
- **the discovery of new continents** and their subsequent conquest in the 16th and 17th centuries gives European countries access to natural resources and labour
- the **Industrial Revolution**, starting with the invention of James Watt's steam engine, enables the industrialized mass production of goods which is based on the constant input of resources, e.g. from overseas colonies
- in the **19th century colonialism and imperialism** is at its peak, leading to the growth of Western economic power and dominance, but also dramatic and long-lasting social and economic problems in the colonised countries which linger to this day

Global players – and the consequences

- **multinational companies** (or mega corporations) play an important role in the international economy: they often have powerful influence on local economies, international relations and even politics (➔ lobbying)
- **many multinational companies are criticized** due to lax environmental standards, bad labour standards (e.g. sweatshops in

developing countries, control of tariffs → unfair wages), marginalization of local businesses/markets

- many multinationals hold **patents** (e. g. Siemens, Adidas) in order to prevent the rise of competitors
- examples of **influential multinational corporations** are: Exxon-Mobil, Wal-Mart, McDonald's, General Electric, Boeing, Microsoft and British Petrol
- the United Nations declare **2005 the International Year of Microcredit**; microloans are designed to spur entrepreneurship in developing countries and gain acceptance in the mainstream finance industry as a source of future growth

Energy – reserves and consumption

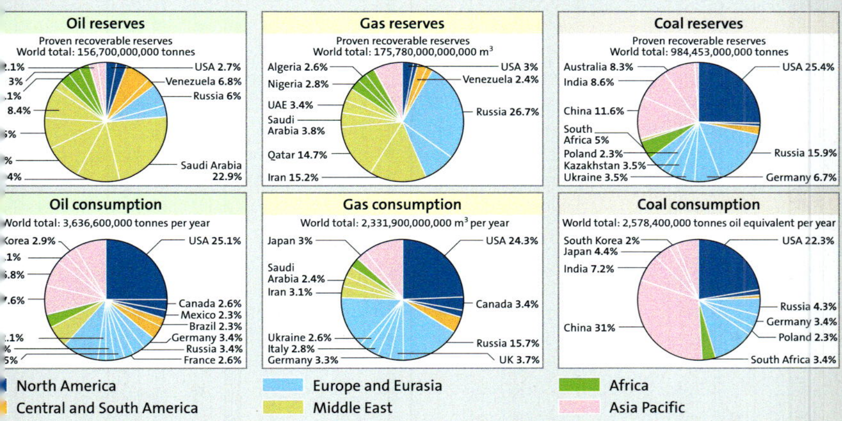

Globalisation

Globalisation is the **intergration/ connection of regional economies** through a global network based on communication, transportation and trade.

Globalisation cube with the leading global economies and corporations

defining features	threats/dangers	opportunities	impacts
• communication technology • resources • modern means of transportation • multinational corporations • liberalization of trade barriers • reorganization of work • mass tourism	• ecological exploitation of countries that provide the resources • exploitation of workers • growing inequity • scramble for resources can lead to conflict • growing environmental problems • unprecedented growth of mega corporations • rising unemployment for unskilled workers • terrorism due to open borders	• exchange/circulation of ideas • exchange of culture • exchange of language • generating capital • investment in poorer countries • higher living standard in the developing countries • innovation through the exchange of ideas • free trade of goods • mutual support and understanding due to stronger interdependencies	• cultural imperialism/ Westernization of the world • rising migration • fear of being overrun → restrictions on immigration • mutual influence of cultures on each other • outsourcing of work

Globalisation index, 2006

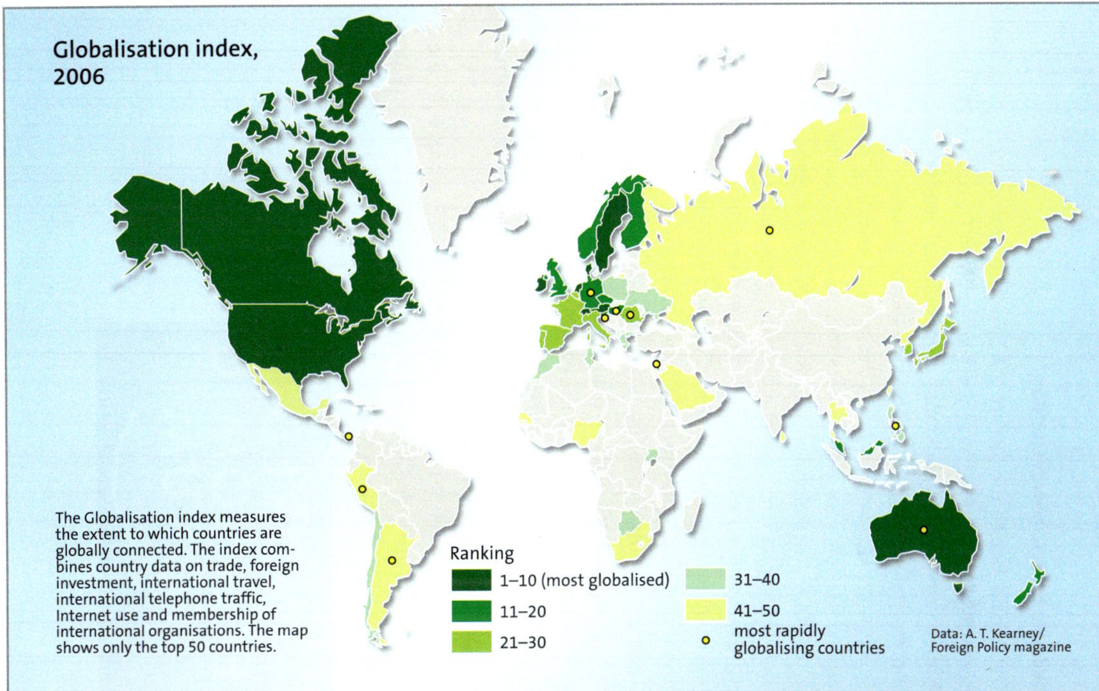

The Globalisation index measures the extent to which countries are globally connected. The index combines country data on trade, foreign investment, international travel, international telephone traffic, Internet use and membership of international organisations. The map shows only the top 50 countries.

World Trade

World Economic Forum

The **World Economic Forum** (WEF), founded in 1971, is a Swiss nonprofit foundation that meets annually in Davos, and **brings together international business and political leaders, intellectuals and journalists to discuss pressing global issues**.
Besides its economic focus, the annual meeting has become a neutral platform for political leaders to resolve political differences. In 2008, Microsoft founder Bill Gates gave a keynote speech on "creative capitalism", which combines generating profits and solving the world's inequities by using market forces to address the needs of the poor worldwide. The participants are considered a global elite – a think tank of internationally-oriented experts, including a group of "Young Global Leaders" consisting of under-forty-year-old leaders from all around the world and representing a wide range of disciplines and sectors.
WEF has also **launched several global initiatives**, e.g. the **Global Health Initiative**, the **Global Education Initiative** and the **Partnering Against Corruption Initiative**.
However, there is heavy criticism as well: WEF, along with the G8 and the World Trade Organisation, are viewed as a "mix of pomp and platitude" by anti-globalisation activists and many NGOs.

Further economic forums

- **The Group of Eight (G8):** France, Germany, Italy, Japan, the United Kingdom, the United States, Canada and Russia

This group has occasionally been expanded, e. g.:

- **Outreach Five (O5):** plus Brazil, China, India, Mexico and South Africa
- **Group of Twenty (G20):** the 20 major economies of Africa, North America, South America, East Asia, South Asia, Southeast Asia, Western Asia, Eurasia, Europe and Oceania; the group meets semi-annually, and the last meeting took place in Seoul in November 2010.

ɔrld trade cartogram, 2005

size of each country represents its share of total world trade.

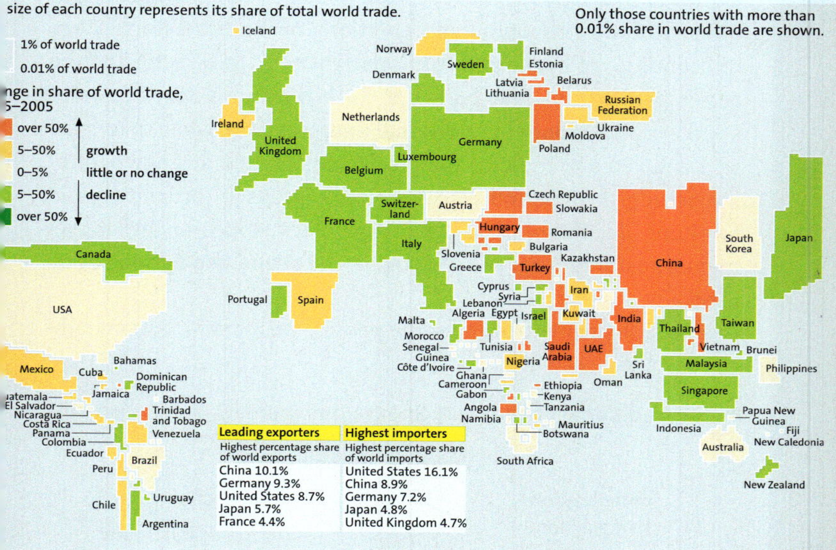

Leading exporters	Highest importers
Highest percentage share of world exports	Highest percentage share of world imports
China 10.1%	United States 16.1%
Germany 9.3%	China 8.9%
United States 8.7%	Germany 7.2%
Japan 5.7%	Japan 4.8%
France 4.4%	United Kingdom 4.7%

Drama and Theatre

Drama

A **drama or play** is written to be performed by **actors** in a theatre, in a film, on television or on the radio. Traditionally, a play is composed of **acts** (units that reflect main stages in the development of the action), which are further subdivided into **scenes** (= sequences of continuous, uninterrupted action). Modern plays may just present a sequence of scenes. More reduced forms are **one-act plays**. One of the basic elements of drama is **conflict between opposing characters (= protagonist/antagonist)**, or contrasting ideas, attitudes and interests. Conflict creates tension and **dramatic action**, which is unfolded in **dialogues** and/or **monologues**. Good dialogues or monologues must capture the personalities, social positions, attitudes, thoughts and emotions of the characters. **Stage directions** given by the **author/playwright** help the director and the actors perform the play on stage. Such directions may be rather short and leave room for individual interpretation, while others are very detailed and indicate the precise design and arrangement of the **setting** (= time and place), **scenery**, **props** (= properties, i.e. furniture, decoration, etc.), the characters' appearances, movements, gestures, ways of speaking, or the **sound and lighting** to be used.

Drama is the generic term for the genre. The most important subclasses are:

- the **traditional tragedy**, which develops dramatic action like this:

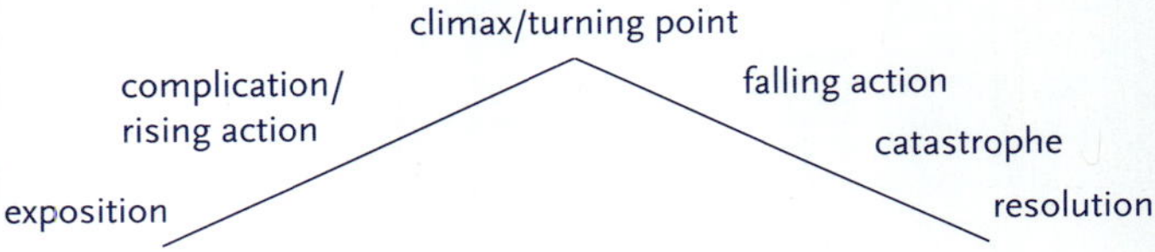

- the **traditional comedy**, which develops dramatic action like this:

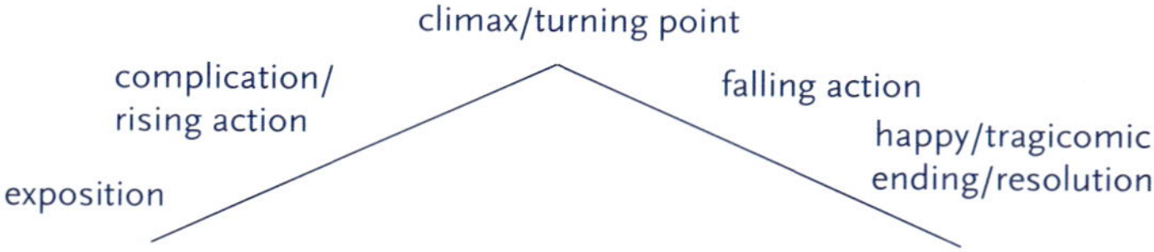

Theatre

Here are some of the important elements of a theatrical stage:

Note: Explanations of the respective technical terms can be found in the Glossary of Literary Terms in your Students' Book, pp. 445 ff.

The Media

In the domain of communication, **media** are tools used to store or transmit information and/or data. The term **mass media** or **public media** is used to describe the sum of mass distributors of news and entertainment. These media include **print media,** such as books, **electronic media,** such as TV, radio and the **digital media,** like the Internet, mobile phones, and so on. Johannes Gutenberg, who perfected the printing press with movable types in 1454, is considered the originator of "print media". Today, modern communication media facilitate the so-called **"many-to-many communication"** (e.g. via e-mail or Internet forums), whereas some more traditional media prefer **"one-to-many communication"** (e.g. TV, radio, cinema). Generally, the purpose of the mass media is to promote businesses and their products, as well as providing entertainment, information and socially-relevant services.

Forms	Usage/purposes/social impacts
Print media	
• books	– require literacy; used to inform or entertain people; more word-based
• newspapers, magazines	– reading usually is a quiet, solitary occupation – possibility of reading texts privately in a critical, creative or extensive way
• catalogues	– easily accessible and affordable media for most people
• publishing	– the distribution of books, magazines, etc.
Electronic media	
• broadcasting	– information, entertainment, infotainment, advertising
• discs, tapes	– storage and reproduction of data, music, etc.
• film (cinema)	– focus on moving images; for entertainment, education, the inspiration audiences; movies can be works of art; can also be highly manipulative

- E-books (electronic books) – texts can be cross-referenced or annotated more easily; more books can be stored; texts can be animated; requires access to an electronic device and software
- Internet – a more interactive form of mass media; almost everything has become accessible via the Internet; global connection of people; forum for business, entertainment, information, education; danger of being spied on and manipulated; reliability and authenticity of data is difficult to verify
- blogs (web logs) – an interactive format; involves the creation of an individual website to exchange commentaries on or descriptions of events, films or graphics/photos
- podcasts – digital audio files; can be used for playback on portable media players; e.g. music, music videos; used for entertainment or information
- World Wide Web – accessible through the Internet; hypertext documents offer a huge variety of texts, images, information, videos, etc.; anyone with a website is able to address a global audience
- social networking (e.g. Facebook, MySpace, etc.) – virtual platforms to build online communities for social interaction; means to connect friends and share information; danger of giving out too much private information and therefore great danger of misure of these data
- mobile phones – used for communication and the exchange of information; trend towards entertainment → mobile music, diverse ringtones, MP3 files, music videos, etc. are available: SMS text messaging is highly popular; TV access; games
- publishing, e-publishing – the activity of making information available to the public; e.g. the distribution of books, magazines, musical works, software, etc.
- video games – mostly used for entertainment; can be played alone or networked with others; often controversial due to claims that they are too violent, sexually offensive, etc.

personal media → non-mass media: person-to-person communication
- telephony – voice communication over distances; Internet protocol (IP) telephony
- mail (post) – physically sent and delivered through the postal system globally; in many countries, private companies now compete with the government's postal service; federal laws guarantee the privacy of the letters/documents sent

The Press

An overview of different newspaper and magazine formats

newspapers	characteristics	tips on vocab
Quality newspapers/broadsheets* *The Times; The Guardian; The New York Times; The Independent; The Financial Times; Daily Telegraph; International Herald Tribune; The Scotsman; The Wall Street Journal; The Observer; USA Today; The Chicago Tribune; The Washington Post; The Los Angeles Times, etc.*	• usually in larger formats and typically with more pages • headlines on the front page are smaller in size and more informative and factual • proportionally more text than photos and in smaller print • more informative/credible coverage • articles are in-depth, present facts, dates/numbers/statistics; are more balanced • use of quotations from credible people • language is more objective/ precise/ elaborate/formal • information is based on serious research; analysis; hard news • objectivity through a variety of perspectives and credible sources • offer critical comments on issues	■ to publish a newspaper edition/copy ■ accuracy ■ informative (-ness) ■ visual material ■ thought-provoking ■ ironic/ satirical ■ column ■ to cover a subject/ topic ■ editorial ■ to generate sth. ■ source of information ■ to be in/to hit the headlines ■ headline-grabbing ■ sophisticated ■ special feature ■ current affairs ■ to focus on sth.
Tabloids/"popular newspapers"/ "supermarket tabloids"* *The Sun; Daily Star; The Daily Express; Daily Mirror; The Daily Mail; Chicago*	• smaller formats and fewer pages • use of banner headlines in bold type • more sensationalist and play on people's emotions • often one-sided and exaggerated reporting • no sharp line between fact and fiction, fact and opinion	■ to skim a newspaper ■ entertaining ■ biased ■ prejudiced ■ gossip ■ attention-grabbing ■ to hound sb. ■ to invade sb.'s privacy ■

Sun-Times; New York Post, World Weekly; Examiner; Newsday; Globe, etc.	• use of subjective, often informal language to appeal to the readership's emotions • often lack of reliable sources of information • doubtful/dubious/debatable sources of information • focus on 'less serious' content, e.g. crime stories, celebrities, etc.	exaggeration/to exaggerate ■ superficial/superficiality ■ inaccuracy ■ (political) leanings
Magazines/ periodicals* *TIME; Esquire; Cosmopolitan; Reader's Digest; Newsweek; Forbes; O – The Oprah Magazine; People; Harper's Magazine; The New Yorker, etc.*	• periodical publications • published (bi-)weekly, monthly, etc. • printed in colour on glossy paper • financed by advertising • two broad categories: consumer magazines and business magazines • often contain cartoons/reviews • sometimes essays or preprints of books by famous journalists/authors	■ to incorporate ■ supplements ■ subscription/to subscribe ■ circulation ■ editor ■ publisher ■ compilation of a front page

Important components of newspapers/magazines

- **advice column/agony aunt***: a part of a newspaper or magazine in which a person (not necessarily an expert) gives advice to readers about their personal problems
- **human interest story***: a feature story that presents people and their problems in an emotional way that attracts interest and evokes sympathy in the reader; often criticized as "soft", sensationalistic news or manipulative news
- **letter to the editor***: a letter sent to a publication about issues of concern to its readers; usually appears in the same specific place (e.g. at the beginning of a newspaper or magazine); comments on or is related to a current or previous edition; can be critical or praising (➔ Focus on Skills, Writing a Letter to the Editor, p. 236)

Analysis of a Fictional Text

The 3 basic types of fictional texts

a) **Narrative texts** (e.g. novel, short story, fable)
b) **Dramatic texts** (e.g. drama/play, screenplay/script)
c) **Poetry/lyrics** (e.g. poem, song, etc.)

Step 1: Analysis of the general meaning

- Identify and specify the type of text as well as the theme/topic/subject of the given text.
- Answer the W-questions: who, what, where, when, why?
- Write a summary of the given text of about 150–200 words at the most.
- Identify the narrator and specify what point of view is being used to tell the story.
- Develop a first (general) evaluation of the meaning and message of the text.

Step 2: Analysis of basic elements

a) **Identify the structural and narrative/stylistic devices** and show **what effect and function** they have.
The following grid contains some terminology and tips for your analysis. The most relevant vocabulary can be found in the Glossary of Literary Terms in your Students' Book, pp. 445 ff.

narrator, narrative situation, point of view, mode of presentation	first-person narrator, witness/observer narrator, third-person narrator, objective/reliable narrator, subjective/unreliable narrator, limited point of view, unlimited/omniscient point of view, panoramic presentation, scenic presentation, relation of acting time and narrating time

structure	• (How) is the text structured? • What timespan does the narration cover? • What is the relation between acting time and narrating time ? • Which conflict is the story based on? • How does the action develop – or stagnate? • Are there any leitmotifs?
characters	flat/round characters, protagonist vs. antagonist, minor character(s), hero(ine), antihero, outward appearance, behaviour, relationship to other characters, direct or indirect characterization
setting (= time and place)	scenery, mental climate, basic mood, social environment, atmosphere • Does the scenery/setting itself imply any symbolism? (e.g. thunderstorm = danger, large city = liveliness, anonymity, etc.) • What is the effect on the audience? • What intention might the author/playwright have had?
language/ style	level of speech, manner of speaking, style, syntax, choice of words, inner monologue, chain of associations, stream of consciousness, register

b) **Never forget to quote** from the text to demonstrate the correctness and accuracy of your work.

Step 3: Comment on and evaluation of the text

- Classify and evaluate the text and its message.
- Relate the given text to other texts of the same epoch/time and/or compare it with other texts by the same author that you have dealt with. Pay attention to striking similarities and/or differences.
- Critically comment on the text and finish with a concluding sentence.

Note: Explanations of the respective technical terms can be found in the Glossary of Literary Terms in your Students' Book, pp. 445 ff.

Analysis of a Non-Fictional Text

Step 1: Analysis of structure and content

- Identify and specify the theme/topic/subject* of the given text.
- Identify the characteristics of the heading* (e.g. provocative, ironical, funny, etc.).
- Divide the text into parts and relate these parts to the heading and the whole text.
- Write a summary of 150 words at most.
- Determine the message of the text. Predict the basic characteristics of the text (type).
- Clarify the line of argument, the train of thought* (general structure of the text).

Step 2: Analysis of stylistic devices/use of language

a) **Identify the stylistic devices** and show what effect and function they have.

The following grid contains some vocabulary for your analysis. The most relevant vocabulary is marked with * and can be found in the glossary in your Students' Book (pp. 445 ff.).

register (= *Sprachebene*)	slang, colloquial, everyday English, written language, (in)formal, poetic, sophisticated, familiar, technical terms, scientific, religious, metaphorical
choice of words	denotations*, connotations*, keywords, figurative*/ literal meaning of words, emphatic/negative function of words, euphemisms*, synonyms*, abstractions
style	plain, sober, natural, matter-of-fact, clear, precise, concise, vigorous, fluent, passionate, elegant, artificial, stilted, wordy, colourless, cliché-ridden, snappy, lengthy, clumsy, spontaneous, trite, expressing doubt/certainty
tone	humorous, playful, colloquial, conciliatory, depressive, serious, solemn, ironical, satirical, sarcastic, warm-hearted, aggressive, whining, reproachful
rhetorical devices	alliteration*, anaphora*, allusion*, reference*, antithesis*, ellipsis*, hyperbole*, irony*, metaphor*,

rhetorical devices	paradox*, personification*, simile*, symbol*, understatement, exaggeration*, parallelism*, employment of leitmotifs*, repetitions*, juxtapositions*, (rhetorical) questions*, quotations, enumerations*, appeals, comparisons, digressions from the main topic, grammatical tenses, illustrations, superlatives, personal pronouns (we – they, I – you, our – their, us – them)

b) **Do not forget to include quotes** to demonstrate the correctness and accuracy of your work. This is how to do it:

- When **referring** to an important part of the text without quoting the words, give the page(s) and/or line(s): e. g. *Clinton tells the audience about his jogging with foreign students (ll. 15–19)*.
- You can **integrate the quotation** into your sentence: e. g. *Clinton is determined to establish "an environment of lifelong learning" (l. 54), which means that ...*
- You can **use a full quotation**: e. g. *Clinton starts with the most important point: "First, to help every child begin school healthy and ready to learn." (l. 42)*.
- Note the abbreviations:
  - one page or line: p. 5 / l. 5
  - more pages or lines: pp. 2–5/ ll. 2–5
  - the following page(s), line(s): f. / ff. (e.g. pp. 5 f. or ll. 10 ff.)

  → Note: **Omissions** of any kind are indicated by squared brackets and three dots: [...]. Remarks or **changes from the original text** are indicated by squared brackets: *He* [Clinton] *says ...*

Step 3: Evaluation of the text

- State whether (or not) the text is well-structured/convincing/ effective/appropriate ...
- Discuss whether/to what extent the text/author is able to address the reader(ship).
- Critically comment on the text, and refer to similar texts that you have dealt with.
- Finish with a concluding sentence.

Analysis of Poetry and Lyrics/Songs

Poetry (from the Greek "poiesis" = making, creating) is a type of literature in which **ideas, experiences and feelings are expressed** in compact, imaginative, and often musical language. Poets arrange words in ways designed to touch readers' senses, emotions and minds. Lyrics are a set of words that accompany music, either by speaking or singing. The word *lyric* derives from the Greek word "lyrikos" (= a song sung by the lyre). Most poems and lyrics are written in lines that may contain patterns of rhyme and rhythm to help convey their meaning. They often use **figures of speech and imagery to appeal to the readers' and listeners' emotions and imagination**. The poet or songwriter usually invents a speaker from whose point of view the feelings, ideas, experiences, etc. are expressed. Poems and songs may be divided into stanzas (groups of lines) or sections and can greatly vary in structure, theme and atmosphere.

general meaning/ content	• What situation/topic is presented? • What is the theme; are there any (striking) leitmotifs? • What is the author's/singer's intention; what is the message of the poem/song? • What kind of register of English has been chosen (poetic, colloquial, archaic, slang, etc.)? • What is the melody like (harmonious, rhythmical, tuneful, staccato, etc.)?
formal analysis: a) structural devices	• Examine – the structure of the poem/song (stanzas, lines, (lack of) punctuation, refrain(s), break(s), enjambements, chorus, etc.) – the use of repetitions and/or enumerations/parallelisms – the use of contrast(s)/antithesis – the use of an illustration (= an example to make an idea clear) – the rhyme scheme (e.g. pair rhyme aa bb cc; cross rhyme abab; enclosed rhyme abba) – the use of free verse

b) sense devices	– (How) are objects and ideas/thoughts brought together? – What type(s) of sentence(s) is/are used (hypotactical/paratactical sentences, questions, commands, etc.)? – Are there allusions/references to a certain topic (e. g. nature, city, love, etc.)? – Check on the use of simile (a direct comparison: "like, as"), metaphor (an implied comparison without a connective word: "an ocean of tears"), personifications (something non-human is given human characteristics: "the frosty cliffs looked cold"), or symbols (an object that also stands for some abstract idea: a red rose ➔ symbol of love, beauty). – the use of grammatical tenses – the speaker's point of view – the use of hyperbole/exaggeration
c) sound devices	• Examine – the use of alliteration/anaphora – the use of rhymes and/or assonances (= imperfect rhymes) – the use of a particular rhythm, beat – the use of onomatopoeia (= words that imitate a sound: buzz, cuckoo, etc.) – the instrumentation, beat, vocal/instrumental type of music, vocals, etc. ➔ **Show how these devices support, stress/emphasize the meaning/content of the poem/song (➔ function/effect).** ➔ **Show how style and content are connected.** ➔ **Show how sound and lyrics match and support each other.**
d) final comment and evaluation	• Try to classify the given poem/song (refer to other poems/songs by the same author or authors of the same background). • Evaluate the poem/song (Is the poem/song convincing? Has the author/singer succeeded in conveying his/her message? etc.). • What do you consider to be the final message of the poem/song? • What do you consider to be the effect on the reader/listener?

Analysis of a Political Speech

General aspects of political rhetoric

The purpose of most political speeches is persuasion rather than information. There is always a (hidden, underlying) message involved, often related to certain attitudes and values of the speaker. A political statement intends to affect the listeners by making use of diverse structural and rhetorical devices. In order to understand and evaluate a political speech, one should consider the following aspects:

first (general) impression:	• topic, subject matter, general tone, issues and purpose of the speech
contents and structure:	• salient and striking topics, important aspects • organization of the text, arrangement of parts (e. g. introduction, main part or body, conclusion) • train of thought, composition, line of argument
circumstances of the speech/ political context:	• time and place/medium (e. g. TV, radio, face-to-face, Internet) • position of the speaker (president, leader of a political party, leader of a protest movement, etc.) • audience (mass audience, a limited group of people) • occasion (election campaign, protest demonstration, political debate, informal gathering) • genre and type (presidential address to the nation, sermon, speech at a demonstration, campus speech, testimony)

formal and stylistic devices:

a) language

- keywords and phrases
- word groups/clusters related to a certain topic
- different registers for different addressees (e.g. sophisticated language to address rich and/or educated people, use of dialect, etc.)
- choice of words (colloquialisms, slang expressions, poetic expressions)

b) grammar

- sentence structure/syntax (use of main-/sub-clauses)
- use of grammatical tenses (indirect references to history, future, etc.)

c) rhetoric

- use of rhetorical questions
- use of contrast and oppositions (positive/negative, familiar/alien, near/distant, etc.)
- use of key symbols, slogans, stereotypes
- abstractions and generalizations
- use of grammatical persons (I, us, we – you, they: patterns of identification and solidarity or vice versa)
- metaphors, personifications
- allusions and references to history (American Dream, important political/historical issues, good/bad times, tradition, future, etc.); quotations
- repetitions (alliterations, anaphora); parallelisms
- comparisons, numbers, factual information
- irony, exaggerations, simplifications
- imperatives, emotionally-loaded words
- concentration on essential points vs. wordy elaboration
- insertions

d) manner of speaking/voice

- volume, tempo, stress, intonation, abrupt changes, pauses, rhythm

evaluation:

➔ Comment on the personal integrity of the speaker, the general political circumstances, the impact on the listeners.

➔ Compare the speech/speaker to other political speeches/speakers. Was he/she convincing?

Basic Types of Fictional Texts

1. narrative texts

a) Novels

- are an extended and complex work of fiction written in prose.
- contain a variety of characters, action and a greater complication of plot.
- present a sustained exploration of the milieu, the characters, their motives.
- can vary greatly in form, style and content; one less complex form is the novella (e. g. John Steinbeck, *Of Mice and Men or Cannery Row*).
- have certain subclasses, e. g. the social novel (e. g. Harriet Beecher-Stowe, *Uncle Tom's Cabin*), the coming-of-age story (e. g. Mark Twain, *Tom Sawyer and Huckleberry Finn*, Paul Auster, *Moon Palace*).

b) Short stories

- are written in prose and are shorter and less complex than a novel.
- are mostly confined to one setting, a limited number of characters and events.
- often employ an open plot with an abrupt opening and ending.
- do not put focus on the development of a character but on a significant incident or decisive moment that reveals strengths and weaknesses of characters, mostly presented as a snapshot of life.
- are told from the point of view of a narrator who is created by the autor.
- place maximum significance on the few things mentioned, which are aimed at producing a certain effect on the reader's mind.
- emerged in the USA in the 19th century in response to the development of the newspapers, which required shorter forms of text; Edgar Allan Poe (1809–1849) is often regarded as the originator of the short story; other famous writers of short stories include Ernest Hemingway, Annie Proulx, and T.C. Boyle.

c) Fables

- are a short text in which animals represent human types (➔ the beast fable).

1. narrative texts	• are a form of allegory exemplifying an abstract moral thesis or principle of human behaviour. • are didactic and are intended to teach the reader a moral lesson. • Two famous writers of fables are James Thurber and George Orwell.
2. dramatic texts	a) **Dramas/plays** • are any work designed for performance in a theater. • require actors/actresses who take on the roles of different characters, performing the actions and speaking the dialogue or monologue. • usually contain stage directions included by the playwright, telling the actors how and where to move on stage as well as giving information about how to arrange the stage, what props, sound effects or lighting to use. ➔ Focus on Facts, Drama and Theatre, p. 186 f. b) **Screenplays/scripts** • are a written work, especially for a film or a television programme. • consist of numbered scenes which show action and dialogue descriptions. • have numbered slug lines telling the reader that the story has changed in location and time (e. g. INT. WAREHOUSE – NIGHT; EXT. STREET – DAY) ➔ Focus on Skills, Filmmaking, Students' Book p. 470
3. poetry/ lyrics	a) **Poetry** • is a type of literature that is not prose, in which ideas, experiences and feelings are expressed in compact, imaginative and often musical language. • may be arranged in lines and may contain patterns of rhyme/rhythm. • often contains figures of speech and imagery to appeal to the readers' and listeners' emotions and imagination. b) **Lyrics** • are a set of words that accompany music, either spoken or sung. ➔ Focus on Skills, Analysis of Poetry and Lyrics/Songs, p. 196 f.

Basic Types of Non-Fictional Texts

The 4 basic types of non-fictional texts

1. Descriptive texts:	the author wants to inform in a relatively balanced and neutral way (e.g. description of a landscape, a place, a person, an object ...)
2. Narrative texts:	the author wants to inform the reader about a development or a sequence of events; the report (objectively or subjectively) gives answers to the questions *who? what? where? when? why?* and *how?* and often presents further details. Reports* are often made livelier by fictional elements, e.g. a detailed description of people or the way people are affected by an event, etc. (e.g. travel report, report on the development of a situation ...)
3. Expository texts:	complicated and difficult facts are presented and explained in a matter-of-fact way; the structure pattern of such texts is called **topical order** (= a sequence of points follows a statement of the topic at the beginning of the text (e.g. explanatory notes, scientific reports, factual texts, descriptions of historical events ...)
4. Argumentative texts:	the author tries to influence the reader directly; this text type tends to be more critical and appellative, using persuasive arguments (e.g. commentary, criticism, review*, essay*, sermon*, pamphlet, political speech* ...); these texts usually deal with controversial topics; reasons are advanced for and/or against the matter and are arranged in a well-planned order

Forms of argumentative texts

structure	type 1	type 2	type 3
introduction	Presenting a topic and giving opinions on the problem	Presenting a topic and giving opinions on the problem	Presenting a topic and giving opinions on the problem
↓	**arguments** ↓	**arguments** ↓	**arguments** ↓
main part	supporting facts	counter-arguments and refutation to stress the author's position	argument → counter-argument argument → counter-argument argument → counter-argument, etc. [mainly used in disputes and debates]
↓	↓	↓	↓
conclusion	conclusion	conclusion	conclusion

A non-fictional text* that puts forth a personal view has a **unity of thought**, and usually follows a clear **structure** (line of thoughts*, train of thought*, line of argument*).
Here are some of the most common **compositional patterns for structuring texts**:

listing structure:	**method:**	Enumerating, numbering of facts, ideas, arguments
	effect:	Clarity and coherence through parallel arrangement
progressive structure:	**method:**	Using a clearly-defined starting point; developing on a cause-to-effect or problem-solution arrangement
	effect:	Clarity through unity and logical coherence
antithetical structure:	**method:**	Contrasting and juxtaposing of facts, ideas and arguments
	effect:	Clarity and emphasis through comparison and contrast

Characterization of a Figure in Literature

Fictional characters can be presented in a number of ways. In general, a character in a fictional text is developed through action, description, language and ways of speaking.

Types of characters

relevance within the text and characteristics	
• **protagonist** (the main character around whom most of the work revolves)	• **major characters** (main characters who dominate the story)
• **antagonist** (the person who the protagonist is against; often the villain)	• **minor characters** (less important persons who support the main character(s) by letting them interact or reveal their personalities, etc.)
• **the modern hero** (the average man/woman)	• **dynamic character** (changing and developing, with different traits)
• **the anti-hero** (often dishonest, graceless or inept person who struggles in life; the loser)	• **static characters** (unchanging, often stereotypical)
• **the tragic hero** (e.g. *Macbeth*; person who ends tragically as a result of personal flaws)	• **round character** (three-dimensional, with different and changing facets to the personality)
• **romantic hero** (a character with a strong will and personality who goes against established norms; often this figure experiences melancholy, isolation and unfulfilled and unhappy love)	• **flat character** (one-dimensional, viewed only from one side, often stereotypical)
• **the Hemingway hero** (a character who has been at war, drinks too much, the loner, "cowboy")	

Types of characterization in literature

- In a **direct characterization of a character** the narrator or one of the other characters **tells** the readers/audience what the character's personality is like.
- In an **indirect characterization** the writer **shows/presents** the character talking and acting which reveals the character's personality. Indirect characterization can be achieved through:
  a) **Speech** (What does the character say, how does he/she communicate and interact with others?)
  b) **Thoughts** (What is revealed through the person's private thoughts, e.g. in a monologue, soliloquy, a diary entry, etc.?)
  c) **Effect on others/on the character** (How does the person react/respond to others? Does he/she have any relationships? How do others react to the person?)
  d) **Actions** (What does the person do, how does he/she behave?)
  e) **Looks** (appearance, body language, gestures, facial expression, etc.)

How to write a literary characterization

Step 1: Collect the facts and clues given in the text and move from the outward features and characteristics to the inward nature of the character:

- **personal data** (name, age, sex, nationality)
- **outward appearance** (body, face, clothes, etc.)
- **attitudes/views** (thoughts, dreams, emotions)
- **behaviour** (toward other characters, actions)
- **relationships** (social background, family, friends)

Step 2: Draw your conclusions about the person's character and relate your findings to the text by referring to specific lines. Use the simple present for your characterization.

Step 3: Follow the "introduction – main part – conclusion" pattern in your characterization. Write an introductory sentence that answers the w-questions.

Commercial Correspondence

Business letter – layout

① letterhead with logo, postcode, telephone and fax numbers, e-mail and Internet address
② reference initials
③ date
④ special marking (optional)
⑤ inside address, including street, ZIP code, country
⑥ attention line
⑦ salutation
   – *Dear Sir or Madam* → used if name is unknown
   – *Miss* → unmarried woman (old use)
   – *Mrs* → married woman
   – *Ms* → unclear if the woman is married or not
   – *Mr* → man
   – no comma at the end of the salutation
⑧ subject line (optional)
   – after salutation in the UK
   – before salutation in the USA
   – in bold type
   – capitalized
⑨ body of the letter
   – begin with a capital letter
   – paragraphs are separated by a free line
⑩ complimentary close
   – *Yours sincerely* → most common use
   – *Yours faithfully* → formal, only used if the name of the addressee is unknown
   – *(Best) Regards, Best wishes* → friendly
   – signature, name, position of the signatory
⑪ enclosure (*Anlagen*)
   – Enc (singular), e.g. *order form*
   – Encs (plural), e.g. *cheque, folder*
⑫ carbon copy to Mr Boss

Basic types of business letters

- **Enquiry:** a request for or question about information about sth. (*Anfrage*)
- **Offer:** a voluntary but conditional promise given by a buyer or seller to another for acceptance (*Angebot*)
- **Order:** a request to make or supply goods (*Bestellung*)
- **Reminder:** a request for an overdue payment that should have been paid by an earlier date (*Mahnung*)
- **Letter of complaint:** a request to deal with and solve a problem, e.g. delay in delivery, unsatisfactory or defective goods, wrong goods, etc. (*Beschwerdebrief, Reklamation*)

BIG COMPANY

① *15 Prince William Square*
London 3UP4X
United Kingdom

Tel. +44(0) 007 123 456 789
Fax + 44(0) 007 123 456 7890
E-mail: big.company@supernet.com
http://www.bigcompany.com

② Our ref: TS/MB
Your ref: SG/TS

③ 10 August 2013

④ **URGENT**

⑤ Nice Furniture Corporation
8607 Main Street
Cornerstone, NY 23567
USA

⑥ Attention: Ms Goldwell, Sales Department

⑦ Dear Ms Goldwell

Your Offer of 28 July 2013, for Cafeteria Furniture ⑧

⑨ Many thanks for your offer which our cafeteria team will decide about within the next two weeks.

We are very impressed by the design and quality of your furniture and we are looking forward to cooperating with you.

As soon as we have decided on the details of the refurbishment we will contact you.

⑩ Yours sincerely
Big Company

Tom Sunshine
Assistant Manager

⑪ Enc.: Brochure of our company
⑫ Cc. Mr B. Boss, CEO

Enquiry

An enquiry can be a general or specific request for (detailed) information on a product, service or a credit reference, etc. It can be **written as a letter, fax or an e-mail**.

Enquiry – letter plan

- source of address, e.g. trade fair, advert, Internet, etc.
- description of your company/reason for enquiry
- say what you require e.g.:
  - quotation for goods/services
  - information
- ask for:
  - sales material, brochures, etc.
  - samples
  - representative's/agent's visit
  - demonstration or presentation
- ask about:
  - terms of delivery
  - delivery date/period
  - terms of payment
- give references as appropriate
- polite ending
- enclosure(s)

Useful phrases

- We recently visited your exhibition ... and were most impressed by ...
- We have seen your advertisement ... and have noted with interest ... we would be most grateful ...
- As a leading importer of ... we feel that your unique product will complete our selection of ...
- Please send us an illustrated colour brochure, your current price list ... and details of your discounts ...
- Please also state your terms of delivery and payment ...
- Should you require references, feel free to contact ... we will be pleased to provide you with any information that you desire ...
- Documents or further information may be obtained from ...
- If your offer meets our requirement we will be pleased to place a trial order ...

BIG COMPANY

15 Prince William Square
London 3UP4X
England, U.K.
Tel. +44(0) 007 123 456 789
Fax + 44(0) 007 123 456 7890
E-mail: big.company@supernet.com
http://www.bigcompany.com

TS/MB
15 October 2013

Nice Furniture Corporation
8607 Main Street
Cornerstone, NY 23567
USA

Attention: Mr Johnson, Public Relations

Dear Mr Johnson

Your Stand at the Furniture Trade Fair in Munich

With great interest we visited your stand at the Furniture Trade Fair in Munich and were most impressed by your choice of Lifestyle and School furniture.

Please send us an illustrated colour brochure, your current export price list and details of your discounts for quantity, cash, early payment, and initial orders. Please also state your terms of delivery and payment, indicating delivery times.

We look forward to hearing from you soon.

Yours sincerely
Big Company

Tom Sunshine
Assistant Manager

Cc. Mr B. Boss, CEO

Offer

When you want to write an offer you should use the **common form of layout of a business letter, fax or e-mail** as well as the letter plan. (→ Fos, Business Letter, pp. 206 f.)

Offer – letter plan	Useful phrases
reference to enquiry	■ We enclose your enquiry … ■ find enclosed our offer …
description of your company	■ We are a market-leading company …
description of goods/services	
reference to information or samples, representative's or agent's visit, etc.	■ The enclosed brochure gives you an overview of … ■ we are pleased to supply you with samples …
prices and discounts	We offer a discount of … ■ the prices include an initial order discount ■ the article is priced … each ■ The final price per item …
terms of delivery (e. g. from stock, subject to availability, costs of shipping, etc.)	■ The price are inclusive packing, to send /ship an article by express delivery
terms of payment, e. g. cash with order, 30 days net on receipt, etc.	■ We accept payment by Visa, Mastercard …
validity of offer	■ We guarantee the special offer until …
instructions as appropriate	■ We reserve the right to return the goods if they are delivered late ■ delivery within … days after receipt of order ■ please confirm receipt of this order
offer of agency/exclusive right of sale as appropriate	■ We agree to your exclusive right of selling the products to …
polite ending	■ We are looking forward to making business with you ■ we are looking forward to receiving your order
enclosure(s)	

34765 Lomax Avenue
New York, NY 10034
U.S.A

Tel. +001(0) 212 123 456 789
Fax + 001(0) 212 123 456 7890
E-mail: gingerbread@supernet.com
http://www.gingerbread.com

PS/MB
15 October 2013

The Cake Company
8607 Main Street
Cornerstone, NY 23567
USA

Attention: Mr Miller, Purchasing

Dear Mr Miller

Your Enquiry Concerning Gingerbread Men

We were delighted to receive your enquiry of July 7 about our range of gingerbread bakery items. As a major producer of gingerbread we have been enlarging our variety of products throughout the last 75 years.

We enclose a brochure on our gingerbread speciality goods and will be pleased to supply you with samples if requested.

The current whole sale price for lb 2 selection of gingerbread speciality goods is $10, excluding taxes. New customers are granted a discount of 25 % on initial orders exceeding more than $2,000. Deliveries can be made from stock, subject to availability. There has been a heavy demand for this article recently so we recommend your order soon while stocks last.

Please do not hesitate to contact us if you require further details. We look forward to receiving your order.

Sincerely yours,
Phil Stone
Phil Stone
Assistant Sales Manager

cc. Mr B. Boss, CEO, Enclosures

Order

When you want to write an order you should use the **common form of layout of a business letter, fax or e-mail** as well as the letter plan (→ Fos, Business Letter, pp. 206 f.).

Useful phrases

- We enclose our order ..., please supply ..., I particularly would like to order
- We agree to an exceptional quantity discount of ...
- We request you to send the goods as soon as possible, we request to send the goods as soon as possible ...
- Payment by transfer to your account at ... within 30 days after receipt of invoice ...
- Please arrange the goods to be dispatched immediately ...
- Thank you for your prompt attention to this matter ..., Many thanks in advance for attention ...

389 Delancy Road
Wolverhampton 7OM3W
England, U.K.

Tel. +44(0) 007 123 456 789
Fax + 44(0) 007 123 456 7890
E-mail: happy.toysy@supernet.com
http://www.happytoys.com

LM/MB
25 May 2013

Die Bärenfabrik
Hauptstraße 35
70854 Kleinbärendorf
Germany

Attention: Ms Mayer, Sales Department

Dear Ms Mayer

Order for Plush Toys and Rag Dolls

We have studied your catalogue and export price list sent to us on 10 April and enclose our order no. 3456CP.

Please supply:

Quantity	Description	Article number	List Price	Unit Price (– 20% discount)	Total Price
80	Teddy Bears	T 007	€ 50	€ 40	€ 3,200.00
50	Rag Dolls	R 456	€ 30	€ 24	€ 1,200.00
				Total	**€ 4,400.00**

Delivery to made within 10 days after receipt of order, franco or to our premises.

Thank you for your prompt attention to this matter.

Sincerely, Happy Toys Ltd.

Timothy Sweeney

Purchasing Assistant Manager
cc. Mr B. Boss, Purchasing Director

Complaint (The Seller)

Whenever goods or services are not satisfactory, defective or delivered delayed, **the buyer should inform the seller immediately**. The seller should express his regrets to the customer and investigate the case in order to offer an explanation. However, **complaints should be dealt with politely and factually** on both sides in order to promote goodwill. In general, you should use the **common form of layout of a business letter, fax or e-mail** (→ FoS, Business Letter, pp. 206 f.).

Dealing with a complaint – letter plan (the seller)	Useful phrases
acknowledge receipt of the buyer's letter immediately	■ Many thanks for your message regarding the damages of …
say you are sorry that the buyer is dissatisfied	■ We are dismayed to hear that the goods were damaged …
say that the matter will be/ has been/is being dealt with	■ We are now looking into the matter …
ask for more time to investigate the complete	■ We would very much appreciate it if you would let us have a few more days to investigate …
request proof	■ We are now waiting for the freight forwarder's report …
explain the reasons …	Obviously the problem has come about … ■ it might have happened …
apologise for ….	■ We do, of course, very much regret …
explain that you are not at fault/partly at fault/at fault	■ The goods were roughly handled in transit, the damage can have only been caused after the goods left our premises…
suggest a solution (discount, return, exchange, etc.)	■ We have contacted the … company ■ as a gesture of goodwill, we are offering replacement …
polite ending	■ We hope our suggestion meets your approval ■ we are sure the matter will be settled to the satisfaction of all parties concerned ■ we look forward to doing further business with you …

3065 Garden Road
Brighton 4M5L3P
England, U.K.

Tel. +44(0) 007 123 456 789
Fax + 44(0) 007 123 456 7890
E-mail: happy.garden@supernet.com
http://www.happygarden.com

DM/MB
25 June 2013

Fun Flowers Co.
15 Lady Diana Court
London 3UP4X
England, U.K.

Attention: Ms Simpson, Managing Director

Dear Ms Simpson

Your Order No. BG-007-1234 dated 15 June ... for 500 Red Roses
Your Letter dated 24 June ...

We have just received your letter concerning the above-mentioned order and are dismayed to hear that the delivered roses are the wrong colour.
We are now looking into the matter and have already contacted the nursery that cultivated and delivered the roses to us.

We very much regret that this should have happened and agree to request to sell the pink roses to you at a 30% reduction.

Unfortunately we have to inform you that a delivery of 500 red roses until 27 June is not possible. Alternatively, we can offer you 200 red roses and 300 white roses at a special price and the express delivery on 26 June ... at our expenses.

We are sure that the matter will be settled to the satisfaction of all parties concerned and look forward to your answer.

Yours sincerely,

Happy Garden Nurseries

Diane Marigold
Managing Director

Complaint (The Buyer)

Whenever goods or services are not satisfactory, defective or delivered delayed, **the buyer should inform the seller immediately**. The seller should express his regrets to the customer and investigate the case in order to offer an explanation. However, **complaints should be dealt with politely and factually** on both sides in order to promote goodwill. In general, you should use the **common form of layout of a business letter, fax or e-mail** (→ FoS, Business Letter, p. 206).

Making a complaint – letter plan (the buyer)

- confirm receipt of the goods/performance of services
- say what is wrong
- refer to or enclose proof as appropriate
- ask for an explanation
- consequences for the buyer's company
- return the goods to the seller as appropriate
- polite ending
- enclosure(s)

Useful phrases

- Thank you for the delivery of ... which we received yesterday ...
- Unfortunately the above-mentioned goods were badly damaged in transit ...
- We enclose photographs of the damage for your information ...
- We believe that the goods were poorly packed and roughly handled ...
- ... the goods are consequently unsaleable ... we cannot sell .... and would like to return ...
- We look forwards to receiving your comments ...

15 Lady Diana Court
London 3UP4X
England, U.K.

Tel. +44(0) 007 123 456 789
Fax + 44(0) 007 123 456 7890
E-mail: fun.flowers@supernet.com
http://www.funflowers.com

LS/MB
24 June 2013

Happy Garden Nurseries
3065 Garden Road
Brighton, 4M5L3P
England, U.K.

Attention: Ms Marigold, Managing Director

Dear Ms Marigold

Our Order No. BG-007-1234 dated 15 June ... for 500 Red Roses

The above-mentioned roses were delivered to us today and on opening the boxes we found that most of the roses had the wrong colour (pink) and can consequently not be used for wedding ceremony as they do not match the overall decoration.

We enclose photographs of the roses for your information.

Needless to say we cannot use and sell the roses at the price agreed and will only keep them if a reduction in price of 30% is granted. Additionally we request you to urgently deliver the required 500 red rose until 27 June by express delivery at your expenses in order to accomplish our contract concerning the wedding ceremony decoration.

We look forward to receiving your comments on this matter in the very near future.

Yours sincerely,

Fun Flowers Co.

Lilly Simpson
Managing Director

Enc.: Photographs of the delivered roses

Giving a Speech

Why giving a speech is good for you

- You learn to **speak effectively** in **different situations** and to audiences of **different backgrounds** and **levels of knowledge** and improve your **general speaking abilities**.
- The ability to speak well enough to **interest, influence or persuade people** is a major asset for your future life.
- You **gain self-confidence** by learning to overcome and manage nervousness and excitement.
- You learn **different techniques** of **using and varying your voice** and tone of speaking.
- You learn to control your **body language** and to **choose the right words** in the respective situation.
- You learn to **listen to people** to speak more effectively to them.

Non-verbal communication

The **major tools** you will use as you speak are **your voice and your body language**. Here are some aspects that help you to check yourself and be better prepared for a speech:

Voice:

- Is my voice (too) loud or (too) soft or is it monotonous?
- Do I speak (too) slowly or (too) quickly?
- Do I articulate clearly or do I mutter?
- Will my accent be a problem for my audience?
- Do I run out of air and gasp when I speak?

→ Try to **speak naturally and clearly**, and check (ask your audience) whether you can be heard.

→ **Do not shout**, because this is hard on the voice and uncomfortable for the listener.

→ Go in advance to the room in which you will be speaking and **familiarize yourself with its layout**.

→ Try to **vary your speech** by raising and lowering your voice, stressing and emphasizing keywords.

→ **Mark up your script or notes** using a highlighter on the points you want to stress.

→ **Make pauses in your talk** and give the audience and yourself time to think and reflect (e.g. use visual aids).

Body language:

- Do I rush into the room or walk in confidently and determined?
- Do I look down, hunch my shoulders and shuffle my feet (lacking confidence)?
- Do I look at the audience and smile at them before starting to speak (eye contact)?
- Do I look comfortable and businesslike?
- Do I look (too) casual or nervous?
- Do I use my hands and arms to reinforce a detail of my speech?

→ **Smile at the audience** to make them feel welcome and to **establish a good relationship**.

→ **Tell yourself that it will be a good, friendly and supportive audience** to calm yourself down.

→ **Show a cheerful**, enthusiastic **and positive state of mind**.

→ **Make eye contact** with the audience; it gives the audience the impression that you are trustworthy and honest.

→ **Put your script at the right distance** for **reading and look** up at the audience occasionally.

→ Do **not fold your arms in front of you** or put your hands in your pockets.

→ **Open your hands to show an outgoing and friendly nature** – a clenched fist indicates aggression.

→ Do not move backwards and forwards all the time while talking – you will make the audience nervous and distract them.

→ **At the end** of your speech, **leave the audience with a smile** and do not flop back in your chair with a look of exhaustion or irritation. Do not forget: The last impression will stay in the audience's mind!

Job Interview

"Well, I guess a master's degree is a master's degree, even if it *is* in skateboarding."

How to prepare yourself for the interview

- **Research** the company where you will have the interview, e.g.
  – the company's history and background (founder, etc.),
  – make sure to use the company's correct name,
  – the company's range of products and/or services.
- **Think of possible questions** you might be asked and **prepare suitable answers** (cf. Students' Book, p. 79).
- **Rehearse a job interview** with a friend and have them ask you questions (that you have prepared *and* surprise questions).
- **Evaluate** the "mock interview" with your friend:
  – Which answers turned out well and which ones need to be improved?
  – What impression did your friend have of you (body language, nervousness, friendliness, etc.)?
- Think of **questions that you want to ask** the interviewer. Your questions should reveal that you already know something about the company and its management and structure (cf. Tips on vocab below).
- **Dress** nicely, neatly and **appropriately**.
- **Arrive early** so that you have time to collect your thoughts and appear calm and relaxed.

Tips on vocab

the company's corporate culture/identity ■ challenges/innovations for the future ■ plans for future expansion ■ approach taken towards managing employees ■ management philosophy

What to do during the interview

- **Smile and maintain eye contact** with your interviewer. **Be positive** and try to convey that you are enthusiastic and energetic.

- If the interviewer tries to lighten the interview with some **small talk, be prepared to chat** with him/her.
- **Speak clearly and slowly.** Do not rush through your answers and give yourself time to think before you answer. You do not want to convey the impression of being thoughtless or superficial.
- Do not hesitate **to ask the interviewer to repeat** or explain his/her question.
- **Do not simply answer questions with "yes", "no" or "I don't know".** The interview is your chance to express your thoughts and convince the interviewer that you are the best choice for the job. But: be careful not to talk too much – **keep your answers clear and concise**.
- If there is still time (or the interviewer asks you to do so) **you can ask the questions** that you prepared.
- **Thank your interviewer** at the end.

Tips on vocab

I didn't have any difficulty finding you. The map your secretary sent me was very helpful. ■ As you can see from my CV ... ■ ... perhaps you would like me to tell you something about my experience in ... ■ Is there anything specific you would like to know about me? ■ Could you tell me more about ...? ■ Thank you very much for seeing me. ■ Thank you for your time.

After the interview

- After a short time (ca. 2 weeks), **send a follow-up mail/letter** thanking your interviewer.
- **Express your interest** in the company again.
- Ask politely **when you can expect a reply**/a decision.

Tips on vocab

How shall we proceed? ■ When can I expect to hear from you? ■ When will a decision be made? ■ When are you likely to make a decision? ■ I had an interview for the position of a ... three weeks ago and would like to enquire whether a decision has been taken yet.

The structure of a job interview

Most job interviews (screening, follow-up or single and group interviews) follow a similar structure that an applicant can expect and get prepared to. However, sometimes the questions may (slightly) vary or the applicant may be expected to answer them in more or less detail.

Applicant	**Interviewer/company representative**
Starting a conversation	
Nice to see/meet you ... How are you doing? (more casual) How do you do? (formal)	Good morning, Mr/Ms ... How are you? How do you do? Nice to see/meet you ...
Small talk/"warming up"	Did you find us alright? How did you get here? How was your trip?
Oh, yes, thank you. The map which your secretary e-mailed me was very helpful. Oh, yes, thank you. The navigation system I used had no problems in finding your company.	So, you are from ... ? What a beautiful area! I went there last year ... We visited ....
Introducing yourself	So, tell me about yourself! How would you describe yourself?
As you can see from my CV I am ... years old and I was born in ... Apart from German and English I speak fluent Spanish and ... I graduated from ... with a ... degree in Economics. Since you can read all this in my CV perhaps you would like me to tell you something you cannot read there. Is there anything specific you would like to know about me?	Why do you want this job? What do think qualifies you for this job? In what way is your education/ work experience important to this job? Why do you want to work at this company?

This is not only a fine opportunity, but this is a company where my qualifications can make a difference.
I want this job because it seems tailored to me competencies, which include ...
This company is internationally known for its ..., and my experience in marketing/ production ... has me intrigued by the opportunity this position presents.

What are your goals for the future?

My long-term goals involve growing with a company where I can continue to learn ...
Once I gain additional experience, I would like to move on from ... position to management ...

How do you handle stress and pressure?
What are your main strengths?
What are you particularly proud of?
What motivates you the most?

I react to situations rather than stress. That way, thus situation is handled and doesn't become stressful.
Prioritizing my responsibilities so I have a clear idea of what needs to be done when, has helped me effectively manage pressure on the job.

The company's philosophy ... services ...

Well, as you might know, our company is internationally known for ... and we have expanded gradually ... until we are proud of saying that we are the leading producer of ... today ...

Could you expand on that?
Could you tell me more about the company's performance on ...?

In what way would you change our company?

I believe that the international success of the company could be further improved by ...
Although the company is known for its commitment to ... I would like to further focus on ... and improve ...

How much salary do you think is appropriate for this position?
What was your previous salary?
What salary do you have in mind?
Would you be willing to begin for less?

In my last position as ... I earned ... I'm sure you understand that I would not like to go beneath that level.
Before we talk about the salary, maybe we could discuss further job responsibilities?
I propose to adjust my salary after the training period. Would you agree?
I propose a salary of .... Would this fit into your company's salary range?

Your questions

Could I have a written job description to this position?
Who would I report to?/ Who would be my supervisor?
How would you describe the ideal candidate for this position?
What are the goals you have set for this position in the coming year?
What challenges does your company face?
How would you describe your management style/your management philosophy?
What else can I tell you to help make your decision?

Ending a conversation

Thank you for your time.
Thank you for seeing me.
How shall we proceed?
When may I expect to hear from you?
When are you likely to be making a decision?
When will a decision be made about this position?

Thank you for your time. We'll be contacting you in ...
We'll be making our decision in ... and will contact you ...
Have a safe trip home ...
Hope you get home safely.

Further phrases ...

Replying/responding

- I couldn't agree more ...
- That's incredible ...
- If there is a problem, let me know ...
- That's the most interesting aspect ...
- I completely agree with you on that point ...
- You've got a point./That's true enough. (partial agreement)

Making plans/appointments

- Sorry, I can't manage Monday. What about Tuesday ... would that suit you?
- Friday would suit me better/best.
- Please give my (warm) regards to ...
- What a shame, I've got to go ...
- It was nice talking to you ...

Telephoning: Making/Taking a Telephone Call

Making phone calls or leaving voice mails in a foreign language requires planning. However, most phone calls and messages follow a certain pattern and can be prepared in advance.

Telephone phrases

Caller	Operator	Person you want to speak to
Getting through to the right person		
(Dials the number ...)	Good morning, Flower Exports Limited. Can I help you?	
Good morning, could I speak to ... in sales, please?	Yes, sir/madam, I'll put you through.	Hello. Sales department. Hello, can I help you?
Asks who is calling ...		
(Dials the number ...)	Good morning, Flower Exports Limited. Can I help you?	
Good morning, could I speak to ... in sales, please?	Who shall I say is calling, please?	
This is ... from Happy Flower in Germany.	Putting you through now, sir/madam.	Hello ... . Sales department ... can I help you?
The person is not available ...		
(Dials the number ...)	Good morning, Flower Exports Limited. Can I help you?	
Good morning, could I talk to ... in sales, please?	I'm sorry, he's/she's not available at the moment. Can I take a message?	

Will you tell her ... from Happy Flower in Germany, phoned, please and ask her to phone me back?	Yes, sir/madam. I'll pass the message on to her.	
Thank you. Good-bye.	Bye.	
Without an operator ...		
(Dials the number ...)		Hello. Flower Exports Limited, sales department.
Good morning, this is ... from Happy Flower in Germany. Could I speak to ... in sales, please?		Speaking. Hello, it's ... speaking. How are things? Hello, Mr/Ms ... What can I do for you? Just a moment. I'll put you through. Just a moment, I'll get him/her ...

Caller	Other person
Small-talk before giving the reason for calling ...	
Hello, Jill, how are things?	Fine, how about you?
Fine./Great!/Not too bad./ Can't complain./Could be better ...	Good.
We've got a lot at the moment. We're snowed under. (casual) We're up to our eye in work. (casual)	Oh, I see. Oh, really ...
How about you? How are things at your end?	Fine./Great!/etc.
The reason for calling ...	
	Now what can I do for you ... ?

It's about the last order ... I need some information on ... There's a problem with ... The reason I'm calling is to ask you ... Can/could you tell me ... I'd like to know ...	
	I'm just assessing it on the computer .... I'll just get your file ... All right, I've got that. Just give me a minute, will you? Just give me a moment ... to find the file, will you? It's coming up now ... Yes, I've got it on the screen now ... Here we are ... I just found it ...
Asking for/promising action ...	
When can we expect ... the order/the goods? ... the consignment? ... the document(s)? ... the work to be done? ... an answer?	It's being dealt with at the moment. It's the next thing on our list. It'll take about ... 2 weeks/days ... Not before the end of ... March/the week ... By ... 14 October ... the latest ... Within the next ... 10 days ...
When can you let me know? When can we expect an answer? How long will it take you to deal with this?	I'll get back to you very soon/as soon as I can/tomorrow ... I'll call you back ... I'll let you know ... We're looking into it. We're doing the best we can. I've marked this matter "urgent". Mr/Ms ... is tied up at the moment ... ... is not available right now ... ... is out of office/on leave/off sick ... I've passed the matter on to ... I'm sorry but there's not much I can do at the moment. It's out of my hands now.
	We'll have to wait and see what the insurance ... says ...

Finishing off the call ...

	Anything else I can do for you? Is there anything else I can do for you, Mr/Ms ... sir/madam?
That's all, thank you. No, thank you very much.	You're welcome. You're welcome and thanks for the order. Thank you for calling. We'll get back to you as soon as we can. Have a nice day.
Oh, by the way, just one more thing ... Yes, there's one more thing ...	All right, we'll look into it as well ...
Bye. Goodbye.	Bye. Goodbye.

Further useful phrases ...

Could I have your phone/fax number, please?
Have you got e-mail?
Cold I have your e-mail address, please?
Has your company got a website?/Are you on the Internet?
What's the address, please?

I'm sorry, I must have dialled the wrong number.
I'm sorry, could you say that again?
I'm sorry. I didn't catch that. Could you repeat it?
Could you spell that word for me, please?

I'm sorry, but it's a very bad line. Could you phone me back, please?
Could I call you back, please?
Could you speak a little louder, please?
I'm sorry but I can't make out what you're saying. Would you like to call back later?

Apologising ...

I'm very sorry about that.
I'm terribly sorry about that.
I fully understand the inconvenience this has caused.
I'm sorry but I'm afraid I can't help you ...

Making a Telephone Call

Making phone calls or leaving voice mails in a foreign language requires planning. However, most phone calls and messages follow a certain pattern and can be prepared in advance.

Here are the most relevant steps and phrases:

1. Introduction/Introducing yourself ...

- Hello, this is Susanne/Tom .../my name is Susanne/Tom (more casual)
- Hello, this is Susanne/Tom speaking from Germany ...
- Hello, my name is Susanne/Tom Müller ... (more formal)
- Excuse me, who is this?
- Can I ask who is calling please?

2. Asking for somebody on the phone

- Could I speak to ...?
- Can I/May I speak to ...? (more formal)
- Is Liz in? (informal idiom)
- Can I have extension 335?

3. Connecting somebody

- I'll put you through (= connect you).
- Can you hold the line?
- Can you hold on a moment?
- Who shall I say is calling, please?

4. How to reply when somebody is not available

- I'm afraid ... is not available at the moment.
- The line is busy. (the extension is being used)
- Mr/Ms isn't in ...
- Mr/Ms is out at the moment ...

5. Taking a message

- Could/can/May I take a message?
- Could/Can/May I tell him/her who is calling?
- Would you like to leave a message?
- Can I pass a message on to him/her?

6. Finishing off the call

- That's all, thank you.
- Anything else I can do for you?
- Is there anything else I can do for you, sir/madam?
- Thank you for calling.
- We'll get back to you as soon as we can ...
- Oh, by the way there's just one more thing ...

7. Further phrases

- Oh, I'm sorry. I must have dialled the wrong number.
- I'm sorry, could you say that again?/Could you repeat that?
- Could you spell that word for me, please?
- What was the name again? I didn't catch it.
- I'm sorry, it's very bad line. Could you phone me back ...?
- I'm sorry, I can't make out what you're saying. Would you like to call back later?

Leaving a Message/a Voice Mail

Making phone calls or leaving voice mails in a foreign language requires planning. However, most phone calls and messages follow a certain pattern and can be prepared in advance.

Here are the most relevant steps and phrases:

1. Introduction/Introducing yourself ...

- Hello, this is Susanne/Tom ... (more casual)
- Hello, this is Susanne/Tom speaking from Germany ...
- Hello, my name is Susanne/Tom Müller ... (more formal)

2. Stating the time of day/the reason for calling

- It's eight in the morning ...
- It's three in the afternoon ...
- I'm calling/phoning to find out if ...
- ... I'd like to get to know if ...
- I would like to let you know /to inform you that ...
- I'm calling to ask you whether/if ...

3. Making a request

- Could you call/phone/ring me back?
- Would you mind calling me back?
- Could you tell ... to call me back?

4. Leaving your phone number

- My (phone) number is ...
- You can reach me at ...
- Call me (back) at ...

5. Finishing the call

- Thanks a lot, bye. (more casual)
- It would be nice if you could call me back today/later ... (more formal)
- I'll talk to you later, bye.

Writing a CV and a Letter of Application

Tel: 0221 123456

① Gartenweg 20
54327 Köln
Germany

② 20 March 2013

③ **Your ref: TBS/1234**

The Hole in the Wall Gang Camp
④ 565 Ashford Center Road
Ashford, Connecticut 06278
USA

⑤ Dear Madam or Sir,

⑥ I am writing to apply for the post of a Cabin Counselor. Please find enclosed a copy of my CV.

⑦ Since graduating from the Vocational College for Business, I have gained experience in working with children in various kindergartens and children's hospitals. I have also had the opportunity to work with children suffering from cancer and have experienced the importance of giving more to these kids than just medical treatment.

I would welcome the opportunity to work in one of your camps in my summer vacation and look forward to your response.

⑧ Yours faithfully

⑨ T. Müller
Tobias Müller

Enc. CV

① your own address in the top right-hand corner
② date of writing
③ reference number or keywords related to the position
④ address in full, as on envelope
⑤ Use "Madam or Sir" if you do not know the name of the person.
⑥ introductory paragraph; reason for your letter; start with a capital letter
⑦ body of letter; your qualifications; reason(s) why you want the job
⑧ If you started with "Dear Madam or Sir," end with "Yours faithfully". If you know the surname, e.g. "Dear Ms. Brown," end with "Yours sincerely".
⑨ Sign your name and print it in full afterwards.

Curriculum Vitae

Name	Tobias Müller
Address	Gartenweg 20 54327 Köln (Cologne)
Telephone No.	+49(0)221 123456
Mobile	+49(0)1723456789
Email	tobymueller@web.de
Nationality	German
Date/place of birth	25 July 1994 in Cologne
Profile	A highly motivated and creative graduate from a vocational college with experience in childcare
Education	
2010–2013	Vocational College for Business (A-Level)
2004–2010	St. Jakob Realschule (GCSE)
2000–2004	Elementary School
Employment/ experience	practical work as an orderly; childminder in various kindergartens
Interests	judo, tennis, music

- only refer to your most relevant qualifications or skills
- if possible, you can include references (= people that can be contacted in order to give a judgement of your qualifications, experience, character, etc.)
- enclose photocopies of relevant certificates
- begin with the most recent employment/qualification and work backwards

Tips on vocab

I noted with interest ... ■ I am writing in response to ... ■ With reference to your advertisement in ... ■ As you can see from my CV, ... ■ I am currently studying at ... ■ Having gained a degree in ..., ■ This position interests me because ... ■ I would be grateful for the opportunity to ... ■ I have extensive experience in ... ■ I am available for an interview ... ■ If you consider my qualifications to be suitable ...

Writing a Letter to the Editor

A letter to the editor is a **formal letter** that has **different functions**:

A reader ...

... **responds to an article** in a newspaper/magazine/on the Internet he/she has read and **states his/her opinion on the matter**.

... **expresses his/her criticism or support** of a stance taken by the publication.

... responds to **another reader's letter** to the editor.

... **comments on a current issue** or a problem of public interest.

... **remarks on materials** that have appeared in a (previous) publication.

... **corrects** a perceived **error or misinterpretation**.

Tips for writing

- **Read the publication thoroughly** and underline/highlight key phrases and the most relevant parts.
- Pay attention to the **focus and the standardized terminology** used in **your assignment**, e. g. "Write a letter to the editor and assess the author's view of immigration to Great Britain".
- **Name the article** you are responding to in the first sentence of the body of your letter or in a subject line.
- Include your **name, address and e-mail address (phone number)** at the top of your letter to give the editor the opportunity to verify your identity.
- Since your letter may be edited, **get to the point and be concise** (*knapp und präzise*) and focused. Do not write a lengthy argument.
- Limit your letter to **two or three paragraphs**:
  a) **Introduce** the subject matter and briefly state your opinion/objection (*Einwand*).

b) Include a few sentences (**arguments, examples**) to support your view.

c) End with a **concluding remark** and a clever, punchy (*ausdrucksstark*) line.

Keep in mind that a letter to the editor is a formal letter. Use **Standard English** and write in **a matter-of-fact style**, using clearly structured arguments. Avoid informal and insulting (*beleidigend*) or offensive language and do not be overly emotional.

Start your letter like this:

Dear Editor/Sir/Madam,

I am writing in response to the article ...

- **If you do not want your name published**, state so clearly, e.g. in the last paragraph.
- Example: "*Please note, I do not want my (full) name published with this letter*".
- **Proofread** your letter to check for poor grammar and spelling errors.
- **Submit** your letter by e-mail (if possible) to enable the editor to cut and paste your letter.

Tips on vocab

to have a good/positive opinion about sb./sth. ■ to (strongly) (dis-) agree with sb. about sth. ■ to approve of sb./sth. (*billigen*) ■ to advise sb. to do sth. (*raten, beraten*) ■ to acknowledge that ... (*anerkennen*) ■ to show one's solidarity with ... ■ to argue in support of sb./sth. (*sich aussprechen für ...*) ■ to take a negative view of sb./sth. ■ to refute sb.'s arguments (*entkräften, widerlegen*) ■ to express criticism of ... ■ to call sth. into question ■ to express doubts about sb./sth. (*jdn./etw. anzweifeln*) ■ to protest against ■ to have reservations about (*Vorbehalte haben*) ■ to disassociate oneself from sb./sth. (*sich distanzieren von*) ■ to make remarks on ■ to make observations about ■ to maintain/claim that ... (*behaupten*)

Writing a Management Summary and an Abstract

Summaries are common in all forms of writing and are aimed at **highlighting the major points** of a piece of writing and **outlining the most important details**.
In **business writing**, a summary is called a **management or executive summary**.
In **academic writing** summaries are called **abstracts**.

Management/business/executive summary

A management summary is aimed at informing the executive manager, e.g. about a business plan, an operations plan, an annual plan or a strategic plan. It should be a concise *(knapp, prägnant)* depiction of all relevant facts and essential aspects. Generally, it should answer the questions: what? how? why?

purpose:	• inform the executive in order to help him/her make decisions • focus on business-management tasks, their consequences and correlations • omission of technical details
structure:	• systematic, clear and concise • emphasis on the main points/aspects • readable/comprehensible for people who are not specialists in the matter • best length is a single page
layout:	• cover page (containing the topic, the hand-in date, names of all persons who took part in the discussion/planning etc., the name of the executive the summary is addressed to) • depiction/summary of the results/analysis/discussion, etc. on one page • attachments (e.g. tables, charts, calculations, etc.) • paragraphs and sub-headlines of the major aspects • a final conclusive statement/paragraph

language:	• clear, precise, matter-of-fact • well-structured sentences • use simple present

Abstract

An abstract is a condensed version of a manuscript which highlights the major points of the material in an abbreviated form. Abstracts have a standard form and are rather short, usually only one paragraph, i.e. about one sentence for each of the points below. They must be concise, easy to read and cover the important points.

purpose:	• What is the author's reason for writing? • What is the author's main idea?
scope:	• What is the author's focus in this piece? • Where does the author concentrate his/her attention?
method:	• What kinds of evidence does the author provide? • How does the author try to convince the reader of the validity of his/her main idea?
results:	• What are the consequences of the problem or issue that the author is discussing?
recommendations:	• What solutions does the author present to the reader to resolve the problem or issue? • Does the author recommend action or change?
conclusions:	• Does the author describe a 'cause and effect' relationship or explain the origins of this issue or problem? • What conclusions does the author draw from his/her study of the issue or problem?

Writing a Comment and a Review

A Comment

A written comment expresses your personal opinion on a certain topic or issue. It is a common means used in print media in order to state one's opinion to the readership in a more or less critical way. Take some notes first, and structure your thoughts systematically before starting to write.

1. Introduction
- Make some introductory remarks in which you, for example, raise a question, refer to a current problem, etc.
- The introduction should clarify your topic/concern.

2. Main part – arguments
- State, demonstrate and describe the positive and negative effects of a topic/situation.
- Support your view of the situation by giving examples. You can, for example, refer to or quote famous people or experts on this matter, or relate it to other comparable issues.
- Emphasize the argument by referring to further/future consequences.

3. Conclusion
- Conclude your comment by giving your personal view of the situation/problem.
- Strategically, it is smart to relate your final remarks to your introduction in order to finally "wrap up" the topic and make your point.

→ FoL, Conversation and Discussion, Students' Book, p. 491

A Review of a Fiction Book or Film

Step 1: Plot*/characters*/theme*
- Briefly summarize the plot of the book/film (approx. 150 words). ("Who/where/when/what/why"-questions should be answered.)

- Include the type of film (e.g. feature film*, western)/ book (e.g. historical novel), title, author/director, publishing/release year, edition, special features.
- Briefly describe the main characters* and how they are related.
- Briefly outline the basic theme(s) and leitmotif(s)* of the book/ film.
- Describe the overall atmosphere of the book/film.

Step 2: Narrative/cinematic aspects

- Point out striking narrative qualities (e.g. point of view*, metaphorical language, structure of the plot*).
- Refer to any striking cinematic devices that create/reinforce the atmosphere of the film.
- Mention which actors were chosen for the respective roles.
- Explain what the book's/film's message and the author's/director's intention may be.

Step 3: Evaluation

- Say what you like or dislike about: the plot, structure, directing, camera work, sound, special effects, casting and performance of the actors.
- Explain whether the book/film has successfully conveyed any/ its main message.
- Comment on the actors: Have they successfully personified and typified the characters?
- Consider and quantify shortcomings/weaknesses and strengths of the book/film.
- If the film is a literary adaptation: How well has the story been adapted? – Is there anything missing (in comparison to the novel)? – or in comparison to other books/films by the same author/director?

Step 4: Conclusion

- Is the film worth viewing?/Is the book worth reading?
- Would you recommend the book/film? – What was your favourite part of the book/film?

Writing – Summary/Essay/ Creative Writing

Summary

A summary ...

- gives the **most relevant facts** and the overall meaning of a text,
- must not contain your own thoughts and opinions,
- begins with an **introductory sentence** (name of the author, type of text, title, topic/problem the text deals with, basic matters of the text, year of publication),
- is about 150–200 words long, depending on the length of the text that is to be summed up,
- **does not contain direct speech or quotations** (instead uses reported speech and/or paraphrasing),
- should be factual,
- leaves out irrelevant details,
- should usually be written in the **present tense**,
- should present the events in chronological order (➔ no suspense),
- closes with a sentence that sums up the main message of the text and its intention.

Essay (= literary appreciation)

An essay ...

- is a type of text that is written in a **defined structure**:
  a) **statement** (➔ of the main idea),
  b) **development** (➔ proving the statement by reference to facts, examples, etc.),
  c) **conclusion** (➔ the main idea is re-stated),
- often makes **use of contrast** (i. e. contrasts are employed to give more force to the main idea),

- contains **illustrations** (e.g. experiences, examples from everyday life, an anecdote, a description, etc.) to arouse the interest of the reader,
- employs stylistic and rhetorical devices to emphasize certain aspects and to influence the reader,
- has a **distinctive line of argument**/train of thought → **a clear argumentative structure**.

Creative writing

Before you start writing a text, you **should collect ideas** about ...

- the topic/the main idea (what?),
- main characters/constellation of characters (who?),
- the setting (where? and when?),
- the plot (= development of action → in what way?),
- the genre of your story (romance, comedy, thriller, tragedy),
- the atmosphere (joyful, ghostly, cold, scary, etc.).

→ Give your text a **clear structure**: beginning – main part – ending.
→ Put your ideas in an understandable order.
→ Decide on which grammatical tense you want to use for your story (present – past – future).

Vocabulary and Phrases for Text Analysis

When you are asked to analyse and interpret a text, you should express yourself precisely and appropriately. Therefore, it is important to use a specific terminology that employs **technical terms** (e. g. stylistic devices) and a variety of formulations that make your text more fluent and less repetitive.

The following words and phrases are related to the most relevant aspects.

introduction	the author
• The text deals with/is about ... • The theme of the text is ... • The text is composed of/consists of ... • Three/two ... different parts can be distinguished ... • The first part runs from line ... to line ... • At the beginning of the text, ... • The author begins by saying ... • At the end of the text,/Finally,/Lastly, ... • The first part forms the introduction ... • The main/central/principal idea is ... • In the conclusion, the author states that ... • In the final part, the author ...	• The author thinks/says/believes that ... • According to the author, .../In his/her view ... • The author illustrates his/her point of view with ... • The author makes a comment on ... • The author is convinced that ... • The author's judgements are (un)realistic/not objective/unfounded/well-founded ... • The reader can sympathize with the author's view on ... • The author expresses doubts/questions ... • The author makes remarks on ... • The intention/aim/objective of the author is ... • The author portrays believable characters. • The author gives a detailed/vague description of ...

the text/the plot/the story

- The story is told from the perspective of ...
- The plot is set in ...
- The text is written in an ironic tone.
- The text contains comical elements.
- The setting of the action is unreal/imaginary.
- The action becomes more/less intense ...
- The situation seems quite absurd...
- Suspense is created because/by ...
- The ending of the story is believable ...

the characters

- The main/principal character in the story is ...
- The author characterizes him/her as ...
- He has many positive traits ...
- His behaviour is marked by ...
- Another essential quality is ...
- She shows her superiority by saying that ...
- He is characterized as ...
- The protagonist lacks ...
- As far as his outward appearance is concerned, ...
- She plays an important/a secondary role ...

the structure

- The exposition gives information about ...
- The first scene introduces ...
- The starting point for the action is ...
- The conflict reaches its climax in ...
- The turning point is indicated by ...
- The crisis is in scene ...
- In the last scene, ...
- This play/story has a happy/tragic ending.

the action

- The action takes place in ...
- The action develops in ... stages ...
- The action progresses fast ...
- The scene contains a flashback.
- The action is interrupted by ...
- This is one of the central scenes ...
- The development of the action is slowed down by ...

purpose (of texts)

- The author wants to arouse the reader's interest.
- The text appeals to ...
- He tries to manipulate ...
- He/She wants the reader to become aware of ...
- The text addresses young/poor/... people ...
- It is the author's objective to create a feeling of ...
- The author attempts to influence the reader by ...
- The advert suggests to the reader that ...

vocabulary

- The vocabulary contains many colloquial expressions/technical terms ...
- This word/term expresses fear ...
- This word has a negative meaning/negative associations ...
- This phrase suggests ...
- These phrases belong to the spoken language.
- The choice of words gives the text its romantic/technical/... character.
- These expressions are typical of ...

criticizing the author

- I (dis-)agree with the author on ...
- I do not understand why he/she ...
- I consider it to be wrong/difficult to ...
- This ... cannot be taken seriously ...
- I would like to comment on ...
- It must be pointed out that ...
- This statement contradicts his view of ...
- There is a contradiction in ...
- It goes without saying that ...
- It is essential that ...
- This raises the question as to why he/she ...
- What really matters is ...
- This problem has nothing to do with ...
- This is of no importance/significance for ...

further useful expressions

- To give an explanation for ...
- The author pretends to know ...
- The author describes the characteristics of ...
- The article is based on ...
- The author makes an allusion to ...
- This sentence reveals the true character of ...
- He/She appeals to emotions rather than ...
- He quotes some experts as an example of ...
- The article relates ... to ...
- The text conveys the impression that ...
- The writer establishes a relationship between ...
- The author's theses are ...
- He supports his thesis with ...
- His/Her outlook on life is ...

- As far as ... is concerned, ...
- From this point of view, ...
- Generally speaking, ...
- As a matter of fact, ...
- In theory, ..., but in reality, ...
- He takes a positive/negative view of ...
- The author generalizes about ...
- This is a great simplification of ...

→ When you analyse or interpret a text, you should use **Standard English**.

→ You should generally use the **present tense** when you describe/ explain or analyse specific aspects of the text.

→ Be careful not to imitate the tone or the language of the text – when you write about a text written in colloquial English, you still should use Standard English in order to appear **impersonal and objective**.

→ Try to **vary the beginnings of your sentences** by employing different connectives.

→ Even when you express your personal opinion about a text/the author, etc., your choice of words should be appropriate and respectful. It can be helpful *not* to begin sentences with "I ..." or "I think ..." but to **focus on the text, the author**, etc. (e.g. The article gives the impression that ..., The author seems to intend to ...). This appears much more impersonal and academic.

→ **Do not overdo it by being too formal** or stilted – your text should reflect your view and stance on the matter.

→ Be careful **not to use short forms** (e.g. don't, doesn't, there's, haven't, you're, etc.) in the tasks that are related to the **comprehension, analysis and comment/evaluation** of texts. They should only be used in creative writing tasks, e.g. in an informal conversation, diary entry, or interior monologue, when you are asked to express your thoughts in a rather informal way. However, when you write e.g. a letter to the editor, you should use formal English.

A
administration 139 ff.
advertising 28 ff., 133 ff.
analysis 244 ff.
– fictional text 192 f.
– non-fictional text 194 f.
– poetry/lyrics/songs 196 f.
– political speech 198 f.
anorexia 64 ff.
application 234 f.
art 121 ff., 130 ff., 154 f.

B
business 139 ff.

C
characterization 204 f.
charity (aid) 27 ff.
comment/review 240 f.
commercial correspondence
– business letter 206 f.
– enquiry 208 f.
– offer 210 f.
– order 212 f.
– complaint 214 ff.
communication 39 ff., 129 f.
community 48 ff.
consumerism/consumption 28 ff., 34 ff., 101 ff.
consumer protection 32 ff., 160 f.
culture (industry) 125 ff., 132 f.
CV/letter of application 234 f.

D
demographic change 164 f.
drama 186 f.

E
eco-fashion 99 f.
ecology/energy 103 ff.
economy 184 f.
education 57 ff.
education & social affairs 150 ff.
Elizabethan England 119 f.
Englisch(es) 41 ff.
environment 93 ff.
essay 242 f.
European Union 178 f.

F
family/family ethics 47 f.
finance 139 ff.

G
gender roles 45 f.
genetic engineering 84 ff., 176 f.
global economy 180 f.
globalisation 106 ff., 182 f.

H
health (education) 64 ff.
human needs/wants 166 f.

I
immigration 71 ff., 168 f.
Industrial Revolution 174 f.
information technology 147 ff.
initiation 10 ff.

J
job interview 220 ff.

L
labour policy 36 ff.

language 39 ff.
letter to the editor 236 f.
(lifelong) learning 57 ff., 63 f.
linguistics 43 f.

M
management summary/ abstract 238 f.
marketing/marketing instruments 28 ff., 156 f.
market economy (factors) 158 f.
(mass) media 125 ff.
megacities 115 f.
message/voice mail 232 f.
migration 69 ff., 170 ff.
minorities 69 ff., 168 f.
multicultural Britain 170 f.
multiculturalism 69 ff.

N
nutrition 64 ff.

O
obesity 64 ff.

P
partnership 45 f.
pollution 95 ff.
poverty 110 f.
press 127 ff., 188 f.
professional needs 55 f.

R
recycling 97 ff.
review 240 f.

S
school systems 60 ff.
science & technology 81 ff., 143 ff.
Shakespeare's theatre 118 f.
society/values 50 ff., 116 f.
society/demography 50 ff.
speech (giving) 218 f.
summary 242 f.

T
technology 93 ff.
teenage pregnancy 8 ff.
telephoning 226 ff.
text analysis (vocab/phrases) 244 f.
texts (basic types)
fictional text 200 f.
non-fictional text 202 f.
theatre 186 f.
trade 90 ff.
trade unions 36 ff., 162 f.

U
United Nations 112 f.
urbanization 113 ff.
utopia/dystopia 87 ff.

V
volunteerism 24 ff.

W
world trade 184 f.
work 18 ff., 36 ff., 218 ff.

Y
youth culture 6 ff.